ALSO BY PAUL RAEBURN

Acquainted with the Night:
A Parent's Quest to Understand Depression and
Bipolar Disorder in His Children

Mars: Uncovering the Secrets of the Red Planet

The Last Harvest:
The Genetic Gamble That Threatens
to Destroy American Agriculture

Do Fathers Matter?

Do Fathers Matter?

What Science Is Telling Us
About the Parent We've Overlooked

Paul Raeburn

Scientific American / Farrar, Straus and Giroux

New York

Scientific American / Farrar, Straus and Giroux
18 West 18th Street, New York 10011

Portions of this book previously appeared, in different form, in the following publications: *Discover* May/June 2014 ("Conception: The Genetic Tug-of-War" as "Genetic Battle of the Sexes: How Parental Genes Fight for Dominance in the Womb") and *Scientific American Mind* February/March 2009 ("Older Fathers: The Rewards and Risks of Waiting" as "The Father Factor: How Dad's Age Increases Baby's Risk of Mental Illness").

An excerpt from *Do Fathers Matter?* originally appeared, in slightly different form, in *Scientific American Mind* May/June 2014.

Library of Congress Cataloging-in-Publication Data
Raeburn, Paul.
    Do fathers matter? : what science is telling us about the parent we've overlooked / Paul Raeburn. — First edition.
        pages   cm.
    Includes bibliographical references and index.
    ISBN 978-0-374-14104-2 (hardcover) — ISBN 978-0-374-71082-8 (ebook)
    1. Fatherhood—Psychological aspects.   2. Father and child.
3. Fathers.   4. Families—Psychological aspects.   I. Title.

BF723.F35 R34 2014
155.9'24—dc23

                                                                    2013041946

Designed by Jonathan D. Lippincott

www.fsgbooks.com • books.scientificamerican.com
www.twitter.com/fsgbooks • www.facebook.com/fsgbooks

Scientific American is a trademark of Scientific American, Inc.
Used with permission.

1   3   5   7   9   10   8   6   4   2

To my father and mother,
who have made a very impressive team

And to Elizabeth and all the children

My father's eyes had closed upon the light of this world six months, when mine opened on it. There is something strange to me, even now, in the reflection that he never saw me . . .   —Charles Dickens, *David Copperfield*

Contents

Do Fathers Matter?

Introduction: Cleaning Out the Attic

I got interested in fatherhood in the usual way: I had children. In the 1980s, I had three children by my first marriage—two boys and a girl, who are now grown and prospering. A decade ago I remarried, and my wife Elizabeth and I have since had two boys. When Elizabeth and I had the boys, friends asked whether being a father was different the second time around. I lied. "Well, sure, I've made all the mistakes," I would say. "This time I can get it right." My older children were inclined to agree with the first proposition, but were dubious about the second.

The truth was, I felt no more prepared the second time than I had been the first time. And it didn't take long to figure out that parenting, for me, was still a hit-and-miss affair. I watched myself once again making mistakes—sometimes the same mistakes I'd made before.

The first time around, I'd operated mainly on instinct, confident that love and attention would go far. One of my editors at the time, a coarse newspaperman with tangled white hair, a rumpled suit, and a carelessly knotted tie who favored three-martini lunches, told me that the most important things to do were to tell kids you love them and to

spend time with them. And that's what I did. It wasn't bad
advice, but I came to realize that it wasn't nearly enough.

The second time around, I had more questions. What is
it, exactly, that fathers do for their children? How much do
fathers matter? And what in turn do children do for their
fathers? These are questions for which many people, including my former editor, think they have the answer. Many of
our parents think they have this figured out and are only
too happy to point out our mistakes as we begin to raise our
own families. Teachers, friends, fellow employees all know
what we should be doing with our children, and many of
them are eager to let us know, whether or not we've asked
for advice. If you live in New York City, as I do, strangers on
the street won't hesitate to tell you that you shouldn't be out
with your baby in this weather, or that you should have
brought an umbrella so the baby doesn't catch a cold. (The
link between using an umbrella and catching a cold is a scientific question I'll leave for another book.)

We see this not only in friends and acquaintances but also
in celebrities and popular culture. When Alex Rodriguez of
the New York Yankees was suspended for using illicit drugs
to boost performance, he blamed his fall on his father's desertion. "The event that makes him so remote, so rudderless,
took place when he was 9, when his father disappeared,"
George Vecsey wrote in *The New York Times*. "This is not
pop psychology to explain a man who blundered into the
airplane propeller of adult reality. This is his own theory."

Of course it *is* pop psychology, and it doesn't do any more to
enlighten us than our well-intentioned friends and family.
As is the case with many of us, Rodriguez thinks he knows

how his father's absence affected him and why it might have influenced him to use illegal performance-enhancing drugs, threatening his baseball career. But while he's entitled to his opinion, he can't really know whether any of that is true. Many of us have ideas about how our fathers might have helped or hurt us growing up, but even Rodriguez can't be sure he's right. That's one of the things I hope to correct with this book. As a science reporter, I'm professionally interested in what we *know* to be true, not what we *think* we know. Much of my work as a journalist has had a single aim: to replace stereotypes and half-truths with what scientists have discovered to be true. When I plunged back into fatherhood for the second time, I thought it would be useful to apply that same rigor to our beliefs about fathers. The more I began to question what I knew, the more I found to question. Is infant bonding limited to mothers? Do fathers contribute to their kids' language development? How do fathers affect children's performance in school? Do they have any influence over their teenage children? And do older fathers, as we've seen in the news, pose a risk to their children?

Much of what we think we know about these things is based on misconceptions. It's long past time to clean out the attic, get rid of these myths, and take a good look at what researchers are learning about fathers and their children and families. The short answer is that fathers are vastly important in their children's lives, in ways that both scholars and parenting experts have overlooked.

For a long time, until women began entering the workforce in bigger numbers in the 1960s and 1970s, fathers had a valuable—and often overlooked—role to play in the family. They brought home the paychecks that housed and fed their families and provided a little extra for dance lessons, Little League uniforms, and bicycles for the kids. And while bringing home a paycheck might not seem like the most nurturing thing a parent could do, it was vitally important: nothing is more devastating to the lives of children than poverty. Keeping children fed, housed, and out of poverty was significant.

But was that it? What else could fathers claim to contribute to their children?

As recently as a generation ago, in the 1970s, most psychologists and other "experts" had an easy answer to that question: not much. With regard to infants, especially, fathers were thought to have little or no role to play. In 1976, Michael E. Lamb, a developmental psychologist and pioneer in research on fathers, wrote that the emphasis on mothers in infants' development was so one-sided that it seemed as if "the father is an almost irrelevant entity in the infant's social world." For decades, psychologists had "assumed that the mother-infant relationship is unique and vastly more important than any contemporaneous, or indeed any subsequent, relationships." The attachment to this nurturing and protective adult was supposed to give the infant an evolutionary advantage—even Darwin had endorsed this exclusive focus on the mother, the experts claimed, and who was going to argue with Darwin?

There wasn't much evidence for the irrelevancy of fathers. But there wasn't a lot of data to suggest they were relevant, either. Few had asked the question, and nobody knew the answer. The irrelevancy of fathers had become an article of faith among researchers, and why would any of them question something they *knew* to be true?

Lamb was among the first to start challenging this assumption. Studies were just appearing that suggested that the bond between mothers and infants wasn't nearly as strong as others had assumed, and that the amount of time mothers and infants spent together wasn't a good predictor of the quality of their relationship. Finally, a few researchers who had dared to look elsewhere were finding that "the interaction that at least some infants have with their fathers is enjoyable and marked by highly positive emotions on both sides." This insight was beginning to appear in professional journals only a few years before my oldest son was born, at which time I could have easily persuaded the professionals that, yes, some infants have fun with their fathers, and yes, you will find that highly positive emotions are involved.

I don't mean to suggest that my experiences with my son should have been sufficient to demolish prevailing psychological theories. But didn't any of these researchers have kids? Hadn't any of them seen a father on the sidewalk or in the grocery store babbling, grinning, and otherwise embarrassing himself trying to coax a smile out of his baby? Hadn't any of the fathers among them done the same thing themselves?

It was around this time that Lamb and other researchers began to recognize the important of fathers in child's play. It's now widely understood that fathers are more likely to engage very young children in what's usually called rough-and-tumble play. That was one of the first important insights about fathers' relationships with infants and toddlers, and it came out of Lamb's research. Fathers in some of those early studies were more likely than mothers to encourage infants to explore, and to challenge them. Mothers were more likely to play with toys with their pre–school age children, while fathers wrestled around with them on the floor. A study by Lamb found that infants actually preferred to be held by their fathers—because fathers were likely to play with them, while mothers were likely to feed them or change their diapers. Two-year-olds who wanted to play sought out their fathers more than their mothers. Playing, wrestling, and otherwise challenging children is a hallmark of the involvement of fathers with their children at all ages.

At the same time, researchers started to recognize that infants have relationships not only with fathers but with other relatives and friends, which made sense. Lamb cites an observation by the anthropologist Margaret Mead in 1962 that attachments to others—in addition to mothers—have "clear survival value . . . since the child then has insurance against loss of a parent."

Many researchers argued that fathers often had a negative reaction to their wives' pregnancies and had limited interaction with newborns. But studies in the mid-1970s were beginning to conclude that fathers were excited about becoming parents and were very interested in spending time with their newborns—again, a finding that should have been obvious, one would think, to any researcher who got out of his office and wandered through a hospital maternity ward. On the other hand, hospitals had apparently not figured that out, either, because they were still providing few opportunities for fathers' involvement around the time of a child's birth.

Psychologists and other social scientists, who should have been leading the charge to change prevailing views of fatherhood, instead contributed to the devaluation of fathers. Many researchers believed that because mothers were the primary caretakers, they were far more important than fathers. That prevailing view put fathers in a tough spot. Fathers could hardly assert their importance when they were repeatedly being told they were irrelevant, except as the providers of the family income.

The record shows that fathers were—and are—widely overlooked in scientific studies. You needn't take my word for this; you can do a little experiment and see for yourself. Go to the website of PubMed, the online catalogue of the U.S. National Library of Medicine. Search for "mothers," and see how many studies come up. Then search "fathers." The last time I did it, I got 97,934 studies when I entered "mothers." "Fathers" turned up 15,156—less than one-sixth as many. Every way I tried it, the results were more or less the same. "Maternal" pulled up 279,519 entries; "paternal" called up fewer than one-tenth as many. Until recently, when we thought about the roles of fathers in the family, we relied on hunches, instincts, prejudice, and misinformation, rather than real understanding.

Others have noted the disparity between studies of mothers and of fathers. In 2005, Vicky Phares, a psychologist at the University of South Florida, reviewed 514 studies of clinical child and adolescent psychology from the leading psychological journals. Nearly half of them excluded fathers. Some involved both parents, but only 11 percent focused exclusively on fathers.

In my research, I quickly began running into examples of what Phares was finding: in 2006, for example, Myrna M. Weissman, a distinguished epidemiologist and researcher at Columbia University, published a study seeking to find out whether treating depressed mothers might reduce the known increased risk of anxiety and depression in their children. Treating the mothers did improve the mental health of the children, but the study didn't include any data on the fathers. Could the involvement of warm, understanding fathers have helped the children even more? Could cold or dismissive fathers have made things worse? Another researcher who was studying interactions between parents and their newborns kept a detailed log of a mother's behavior and activity with her infant. When the mother gave the infant to its father, the researcher wrote "Baby given to father" and closed her notebook; the experiment was over. In 2005, at a meeting of the Society for Research in Child Development, I found hundreds of scientists describing research on children, families, and parenting, and only a dozen or so dealing with fathers. Nearly all the authors of these studies began their talks by noting how little research on fathers had been done.

Kyle D. Pruett, a psychiatrist at Yale who has studied fathers since the 1980s, says that even when fathers are included in research on such important issues as attention deficit disorder, autism, childhood depression, and teen suicide, the researchers usually fail to consider that the father might be part of the solution to the problem. "When we bother to look for the father's impact, we find it—always. Not looking at the impact of fathers and children on one another has given the entire field (and the best-selling parenting books it produces) a myopic and worrisomely distorted view of child development, a view with staggering blind spots." The books he's referring to include those by Dr. Spock, T. Berry Brazelton, and Penelope Leach, among others. Pruett's review of subsequent editions shows they have begun to "nod more often in the father's direction," but "in their souls they couldn't get past the old seduction of the sacred mother-infant bond." The dismissal of fathers could not have been clearer. The mark of progress was that most researchers were beginning to recognize the problem and point it out.

This disregard of fathers perpetuates images that are inaccurate, dismissive, and unkind. The historians Elizabeth and Joseph Pleck point to cartoons from *The Saturday Evening Post*, beginning in the 1920s, that depicted father as a bumbling fool who "did not know how to control or discipline his children. He could not cook a meal or put his children to bed without tripping over his shoelaces." That was only the beginning; fathers were charged with more serious offenses than forgetting the kids' homework or burning the meat loaf. Some social critics blamed fathers for undermining national security. They argued that the failure of many young recruits to pass their Army physicals during World War II was a problem created by solicitous mothers and absent fathers, who had made sons too soft, weak, or cowardly to fight. There have been exceptions to this father-bashing: *The Cosby Show* and *Father Knows Best* on television; Atticus Finch in *To Kill a Mockingbird*; Bob Cratchit in *A Christmas Carol*. But they're rare.

Nearly a century after those *Saturday Evening Post* cartoons, cultural stereotypes of the bumbling father persist. In 2012, for example, Huggies diapers launched an advertising campaign that pretended to investigate whether Huggies were tougher than the competition. "Have dads put Huggies to the test!" the ads said. The message was that if Huggies could survive the ineptitude of fathers, they could survive anything. That same year, during the Summer Olympics, Procter & Gamble ran a series of ads in which it looked at the lives of children who had become famous Olympic athletes. The tagline? "Thank you, Mom." Fathers' contributions were being erased even in sports, where stereotypes would suggest that they might be the more important parent.

More recently, in June 2013, Clorox published a post on

its website that began, "Like dogs or other house pets, new dads are filled with good intentions but lacking the judgment and fine motor skills to execute well." Among the mistakes that the Clorox dads made were taking their kids out in cold, rainy weather wearing a summer onesie; letting kids eat off the floor; and propping them up in front of television reality shows. A barrage of blog posts and comments by outraged fathers prompted Clorox to take down its post. Clorox presumably intended to amuse its customers, not outrage them, but the joke fell flat. Many fathers are now quicker to challenge such stereotypes, and it's likely that more advertisers will find other ways to market their products.

Even though the number of studies on fathers still lags far behind those on mothers, the amount of research on fathers is rapidly growing. In the pages that follow, I will walk you through what I think is some of the most important fatherhood research. We will begin with the evolution of fathers, looking at what we know about the family life of our prehistoric ancestors as a way to get a better grip on the role of fathers now. We'll also learn about how our family backgrounds have prepared us to be fathers. Chapter 2 discusses the tug-of-war between the genes of mothers and fathers that begins at conception.

The next few chapters take us through fatherhood as children grow. In chapter 3, we will look at the changes that occur in fathers during pregnancy. Chapter 4 discusses what we know about fathers after birth, with a detour into monogamy in humans and its significance for fathers and mothers. Chapter 5 shows that fathers and infants are far more connected than once thought. Chapter 6 follows fathers as their children become toddlers and start school, and chapter 7 looks at fathers and adolescents, with an examination of the neuroscience of fatherhood and the hormonal changes men undergo in response to the stages of their children's lives. In chapter 8, we look at the risks associated with older fatherhood, which is becoming more common as parents struggle with the demands of both children and work. Chapter 9 looks at what fathers *do*—what they contribute to child care and other family work. And in an afterword, I'll sum up and reflect on what I think I've learned along the way—and what we have yet to learn.

I admit that it's not easy for me to be impartial in addressing questions about the value of fathers. I have a lot at stake here. If fathers don't matter, I've made poor use of my time over the past few decades, wasting countless hours, days, and years on my five children—all for nothing. Not that it wasn't fun. If it served no purpose, it was, at least a plentiful waste of time of day. As far as I can tell, the kids enjoyed those hours, too, with the possible exception of being required at regular intervals to listen yet again to the one Irish joke I know, delivered in a top-o'-the-mornin' accent that surely is an insult to my own Irish heritage and probably to the entire nation of Ireland.

Our failure to acknowledge fathers' importance is now reflected in the shape of the American family. Fathers are disappearing. Fewer American fathers are participating in the lives of their children now than at any time since the United States began keeping records.

However, psychologists, biologists, sociologists, and

neuroscientists have begun to generate solid scientific data on why fathers behave the way they do—and why it matters to children. They are investigating fathers' behavior, the myriad ways that fathers influence their children, and the factors that shape a father's involvement in his family. Along the way, they've discarded any number of stereotypes—or discarded the notion that any one stereotype can explain what a father does. Gone are the father as moral guardian, symbol of masculinity for his sons, and harsh disciplinarian (all father images that were widely accepted and promoted in generations past). Researchers are now showing that fathers play many roles in their families, including those of "companions, care providers, spouses, protectors, models, moral guides, teachers," and, of course, breadwinners, according to one recent study.

This discovery of the father is one of the most important developments in the study of children and families. The findings, appearing in scholarly journals mostly unfamiliar to the public, have escaped wide attention. That's unfortunate. I've spent the past five years looking over the new science of fatherhood, and I've found it extremely useful in thinking about my own behavior as a father with my children. And I'm sure it will be helpful to others.

Too often, public and political discussions of fatherhood—what it means to be a father, and what fathers contribute to their children—devolve into angry rants and arguments. "Although diametrically opposed, the fathers-aren't-necessary and the father-as-panacea camps share one important feature: they present views that are based more on politics than on actual research," wrote noted father researcher Ross D. Parke and his collaborator, Armin A. Brott. "While politicians change their views to suit the prevailing electoral climate, academic researchers over the past two decades have been nearly unanimous in their findings: fathers matter. And they matter a lot."

What does this mean for nontraditional families—single parents, gay parents, or parents who've adopted their children? As I was beginning to work on this book, I ran into a friend at a writers' conference, a single woman who had adopted a child. She asked what I was working on, and when I told her the title of the book—*Do Fathers Matter?*—she immediately said, "Well, of course they don't." For a moment, I thought she was joking. But she wasn't. I tried to explain that while fathers matter, others can help to fill that role, and that I wasn't critical of her choice. I've made my share of mistakes as a parent, and I don't feel in any position to criticize anyone else. I respect others' choices and trust that with very few exceptions, we all try to do what's best for our kids. We're all in this together, and the new findings on fatherhood should be useful to families of all kinds.

When I was growing up, and politicians were treated with more respect than they are now, it wasn't unusual for parents to tell their children they could grow up to be anyone they wanted to be—including the president of the United States. We now know that that is a very loaded statement; we live in a society still riven by racial and economic disparities that makes it far easier for some to succeed than for others. But we also know that an African-American child raised by a single parent, who barely knew his father, can grow up to be president. The evidence shows that fathers make important and unique contributions to their children in many ways. It emphatically does *not* show that the children in families without fathers in the home are doomed to failure, or anything close to that. "We need to help all the mothers out there who are raising these kids by themselves; the mothers who drop them off at school, go to work, pick up them up in the afternoon, work another shift, get dinner, make lunches, pay the bills, fix the house, and all the other things it takes both parents to do," Barack Obama said during his first campaign for the presidency. "So many of these women are doing a heroic job, but they need support. They need another parent. Their children need another parent. That's what keeps their foundation strong. It's what keeps the foundation of our country strong."

We often say that nothing is more important to us than our children. But our personal and societal priorities don't always seem in accord with that professed belief. This book is about fathers, but it is also, importantly, about children. If we envision a future in which all our children have the opportunity to live rewarding lives, then we would be foolish not to consider the role of fathers more carefully. Doing so will strengthen the family, will help mothers, will promote equality, and will create a brighter future for our children. Nothing is more important than that.

ONE

The Roots of Fatherhood:
Pygmies, Finches, and Famine

Fathers who are expecting a baby might work with their wives or partners to prepare the nursery, paint the walls, or shop for a crib. Depending upon their budgets, the male parents-to-be might join their wives in assembling an IKEA bookcase, a global twenty-first-century bonding ritual. But while these activities can get men thinking about fatherhood, much of what prepares them to be parents was done long ago. At least three forces are at work. One is natural selection, which has shaped them to be well suited for fatherhood. The second is their own family's genetic inheritance, which is part of what makes each father different from all the others. And the third is diet and toxins and other factors in men's environments. We are now learning not only how these forces shape fathers, but how and why they can sometimes go awry.

Not long ago, on a tranquil summer night in South Florida, I had an experience that made clear how unusual and important human fathers are. I joined scientists observing sea turtles nesting on a beach. We watched a female green turtle dig a deep hole in the sand, midway up the beach, and drop some 150 eggs, each the size of a softball, into the hole. She then buried the eggs with a rhythmic flapping of her rear legs against the sand and scuttled back to the water, leaving her young to hatch, find the ocean and food, and mature with no parental help at all.

While she was laying her eggs, drops of a clear liquid began to fall from her eyes, as it does from many turtle mothers. Legend has it that they are crying for the children they will never know. We were moved as we stood on the beach, watching. But these secretions were not tears—merely a way to shed excess salt that accumulates in the turtle's body. Crocodile mothers also cry sham tears while laying eggs—which gave rise to the phrase "crocodile tears" to describe sorrowful insincerity.

The truth is, the turtle has no regrets. Her artful use of her limbs to dig a hole and conceal her eggs represents the beginning and end of her parenting. The story is the same for many, many other species. The eggs are untended, and the young that hatch are set free to make their own way. Mothers who give birth in this fashion often produce vast numbers of offspring to combat the overwhelming odds against their survival. While the mothers' contributions might be slight, they dwarf the contributions of males, who scarcely play any part in this primal ritual at all, beyond their brief role in conception.

The circumstances are different for mammalian mothers—but not so different for many fathers. Unlike newly hatched sea turtles, who are hungry and on their own from the moment they clamber out of their shells, mammals—the warm-blooded vertebrates that include everything from shrews to human beings—have a ready source of nutrition from their lactating mothers. The arrangement has a price, though. Newborn mammals often take a long time to mature. The mother's nutritional investment prevents her from bearing other offspring for a time. And, as with turtles, in most mammal species she gets little or no help from the father.

But in the 5 to 10 percent of mammal species in which males help, the family arrangements can be strikingly different. Certain monogamous titi and night monkey fathers are among the most devoted parents in the animal kingdom. They set a standard few human fathers could meet. Titi monkey fathers provide food for their offspring and follow mothers around all day, so that whenever the babies are not nursing the fathers can carry them on their backs. By the end of the first week, the mother's contact with her infant during the day is limited to four or five periods of nursing. The father carries his infant 90 percent of the time. Many fathers lose weight carrying their infants around. The baby monkeys, in return, are very attached to their fathers— experiments have shown that the infants tend to be *more* attached to their fathers than to their mothers. A titi monkey becomes more upset when separated from his father than from his mother. Infants deprived of their fathers squawk more and show a greater elevation of stress hormones than they do when deprived of mothers. And whether it's to be sure that he is the father of her children or just out of affection, a titi monkey father rarely lets his mate get out of his sight.

Human fathers might not show quite the same dedication to their children and spouses, at least in terms of hours spent feeding or carrying the kids. But they are among the most committed mammalian fathers of any species on Earth. There is no example of a human society in which fathers do not help raise the children. Admittedly, some fathers are better at this than others. Some abandon their families for other mates, and some for reasons we can never be quite sure of. But most human males, at the very least, put food on the table. It would be exciting to trace the evolution of fatherhood over the past few million years to find out whether men were always as invested in their children as they are now, or how that contribution might have changed over time. Did our earliest male ancestors put time, energy, and resources into offspring who would be heavily dependent on parental care for years to come? Or did they swiftly resume the search for other willing females, to multiply again and again, increasing the chance that some of their offspring would survive? And if so, when did that change, and why?

Those are questions we will probably never answer. We're not even sure exactly when, in the course of human evolution, males and females began to forge relationships with one another. But we have some hints, sifted from prehistoric remains examined by archaeologists and paleontologists. They tell us that among australopithecines—the earliest members of the human family, who lived 4 million to 1 million years ago—mates were involved enough for males to have provided food and care for infants and protection from predators. Long-term male-female relationships likely began with the appearance of *Homo erectus* about 1.5 million years ago. Fathers, mothers, and children slept together, so children could watch and learn from their fathers, and their fathers could protect them. In the Late Pleistocene period, about 120,000 years ago, men hunted for large game and often had multiple wives. They spent a lot of time in camp between hunts, and were often available to their children. As the Late Pleistocene period progressed, more complex technologies and art forms arose, and we know that fathers helped to transmit that culture to their children. Circumstances changed at the end of the Ice Age, about 12,000 years ago. Foraging and rudimentary farming became part of the subsistence pattern, and women contributed more to the diet, gathering vegetables. Monogamy was more common, and fathers, no longer pulled away from camp by the hunt, had more time to care for their children and grow closer to them.

Many authorities think the increasing size of the human brain, which has grown continuously over the past 2 million years, was one reason that fathers became involved with their children. It's unclear why brain size increased, but it might have been to provide the social intelligence needed when human ancestors began living in larger groups. As human brains swelled in size, the bobble-headed infants who threatened to topple over under the weight of all that gray matter had to be born earlier in their development. If they got too far along in their mothers' wombs, their brains would get so large that their skulls wouldn't fit through their mothers' birth canals, a problem that can put a sudden crimp in an otherwise promising evolutionary path.

But being born earlier had a cost—the infants would need more care. Human children take longer than any other animal to reach the point at which they can find enough food on their own to survive. For those of you who might count calories on occasion, think about this: It takes 13 million calories' worth of breast milk, Cheerios, and mashed peas to raise a child to the age of "nutritional independence" at eighteen. Mothers were not going to be able to manage that investment by themselves. They were going to need help.

•

To try to fill the gap between what we would like to know about human development and what fossil remains tell us, anthropologists often turn to societies whose circumstances most resemble those of our ancestors—namely, hunter-gatherer groups. Contemporary hunter-gatherer groups are still living much the way our ancestors did for almost all our evolutionary history. Agriculture was invented only about 10,000 years ago, and the industrial age is even more recent, beginning only a couple of centuries ago. Before that, humans were hunters and gatherers, so today's hunter-gatherers should be able to tell us something about fathers before the development of agriculture and industry.

One of the most interesting such groups can be found in the western Congo River basin—not quite the heart of Africa, but close. The landscape there is covered with a sweeping emerald-green canopy, broken by occasional patches of sun-bleached savannah. Gorillas, chimpanzees, red hogs, several varieties of monkeys, squirrels, and small antelopes called duikers wander through the canopy's shadows. Elephants and larger antelopes—the sitatunga—keep to the swampy sections near river valleys. The temperature scarcely varies, and the weather ranges from very rainy to less rainy (the "dry" season).

What might seem to be a tropical paradise is actually a tough place to make a living. Hunters quickly discover that animals are scattered and hard to find. Living off the plants that grow under that green canopy isn't easy either; many of them are inedible. The soil isn't especially good for agriculture. Ecologists refer to the western Congo as "marginal" habitat. But it is not uninhabited. Among those who live here are the Aka pygmies, for whom this is home, a place that has been home to them and to their ancestors for so long that they have learned how to survive and prosper there.

The Aka's skill at foraging and hunting with nets keeps them comfortably fed and content, with time left over. You might even say they live a life of leisure. On hunting trips, men bring their families along to help. Wives are there for more than companionship; they help to chase animals into their husbands' nets. The parents can't pack the kids off to day care, so the kids come, too. The hunts are efficient, the families are almost always together, and the Aka men spend as much time with their children as they can.

Barry S. Hewlett, an anthropologist at Washington State University Vancouver, began studying the Aka in 1973. He did not initially focus his research on Aka fathers, but that changed when he briefly left his studies of the Aka to take a job as a health coordinator for a child development agency in the United States. There he began to study the psychological literature on child development. And he realized that the Aka represented something unique. The descriptions of Western fathers' role and behavior were completely at odds with what he'd seen in Africa. He went back in 1984 intending to focus on the behavior of Aka fathers, and that research continues. Hewlett now has a house in an Aka village that he visits every year, for weeks or months at a time. He's also had occasion to practice the things he's learned about fatherhood; Hewlett has seven children.

Aka parents, Hewlett quickly discovered, are different from Western parents. Hewlett observed that Aka infants are held almost constantly by someone, usually with skin-to-skin contact, because the Aka usually don't wear shirts.

Parents and others "talk to, play with, show affection to, and transmit subsistence skills to their infants during the day," Hewlett writes. Infants "are nursed on demand, and attended to immediately if they fuss or cry." Children as young as a year old, Hewlett reports with some unease, are taught how to use machetes, pointed digging sticks, sharp spears, and miniature axes with sharp blades. It's admirable that children are given responsibility while they are young, and taught to use the tools that their parents use. However, the practice of giving metal axes to one-year-olds might not be one of the features of Aka life that we would choose to emulate.

Despite all this attention and contact, Aka families, unlike many American families, do not let their world revolve around their children. "American parents allow their children to interrupt their conversations with other adults; they ask their children what they want to eat and try to accommodate other desires of the children." That's what Hewlett calls a child-focused family.

Aka society, in contrast, is adult-centered. "Parents seldom stop their activities to pay undivided attention to their children. If an infant fusses or urinates or defecates on a parent who is talking to others or playing the drums, the parent continues his activity while gently rocking the infant or wiping the urine or feces off with a nearby leaf." Aka fathers spend 47 percent of their day holding their infant children or keeping within arm's reach of them. According to Hewlett, infants frequently crawl to their fathers, and fathers pick them up because they intrinsically enjoy infants. The babies are even part of dads' nights out. Hewlett watched men take their kids along when they gathered in the fields to relax and drink palm wine. (Try to imagine an American father slinging his kid on his hip before heading out for a drink with the guys.)

One morning, Hewlett watched a father named Yopo who was in bed with his eight-month-old son, Manda, when Yopo's wife left to fetch water for the camp. Yopo put Manda on his lap, humming to him. Manda reached for a twig on the bed and played with it. Yopo sang as if they were on a net hunt, holding Manda on his chest. Manda cuddled up to Yopo's neck, and Yopo put a leaf on his head. Manda squealed happily. Yopo continued to sing and hold Manda for about an hour, even after his wife returned. On another occasion, a father and a mother saw their fifteen-month-old son have a bowel movement outside, near their hut. The father dropped his work—making string for his net—and cleaned up the boy and the ground, using a handful of leaves. The father then sat down, resuming work on the string. His son walked toward him, put a hand on his leg, and quietly watched him work.

One of Hewlett's many interesting discoveries was that Aka fathers do a lot of their child care in the evenings, when field anthropologists often aren't watching. The usual practice is for visiting scientists to observe when it's convenient, during the day. And they miss what fathers do at night. Too many anthropologists conclude fathers do little child care because they aren't there to see it. We can recognize this in our own families: failure to account for what fathers do at night has bedeviled studies done in industrialized countries, too. "Infants in all cultures wake often during the night, and it is my impression that fathers are often involved in infants' care during this time," writes Hewlett. Since psychological researchers don't generally set up observation in new families' homes, they often miss this. They don't know much about the role of the father because they haven't seen him in action, and so they conclude that he doesn't do much.

Hewlett observed that Aka fathers held their infants about 9 percent of the time during the day, but 20 percent of the time in the evenings. This is not all what we would call quality time—the fathers with children in their arms are often engaged in something else. But the many hours fathers and children spend together leads to unusually intimate relationships, "because the father knows his child exceptionally well," says Hewlett.

In the United States, quality time for fathers often means playtime. Aka fathers do not often play with their children "because they can communicate their love and concern in other ways . . . They know subtle means of interacting with their children." The Aka demonstrate the importance of what we might call "quantity" time—simply spending time with children, even if the parents are not always focused on them. Child relationships based on quantity time contribute to emotional security, autonomy, and self-assuredness.

Studies of the Aka and other non-Western societies challenge much of what we think we know about fathers. They show us that fathers can—and will—do more in the right circumstances. It's unlikely, given the pressures of our changing society, that many fathers will have the leisure to spend as much time with their children as Aka fathers do. Still, the Aka give us another view of what fatherhood can be like, and one from which we might be able to learn something about what kind of fathers we'd like to be.

The Aka give us insight into fatherhood from the time of our prehistoric ancestors, but they don't tell us much about how fatherhood might have changed during the past few decades. As I said at the beginning of this chapter, men are shaped to become fathers not only by evolution but also by their own families and their environments. We are now learning that a family's ill health and exposure to toxins in the environment can adversely affect their future children and even grandchildren.

Most of us know that a woman who becomes pregnant should stick to healthy foods, skip mercury-laden fish, quit smoking, and avoid exposure to paint thinners. All of these things, and more, can affect the health of the fetus. That's easy enough to understand; we're never more intimately connected to our environment than when we are in our mother's womb.

The same sort of reasoning suggests that a father would have little or no impact on the health of the fetus, with which he has no physical connection whatsoever. But that reasoning is faulty: research is showing that a father's environment, his behavior, and even his appearance can have a substantial effect on fetal health—and on the health of his grandchildren.

The first glimmer of this phenomenon came up in the mid-1960s. A pharmacologist named Gladys Friedler was studying the effects of morphine on female rats, and she found that the drug altered the development of their offspring. She then tried injecting males with morphine and mating them with healthy females to see if that exposure would also affect the offspring. The conventional wisdom was that it couldn't; that the morphine might affect the males in a variety of ways, but that it wouldn't affect their sperm. But the conventional wisdom was wrong. The rats' pups were underweight and underdeveloped—solely from the fathers' exposure to morphine before conception. Friedler didn't fully understand what she was witnessing. Neither did anyone else; and nobody believed her. She struggled to get funding for more experiments, and colleagues urged her to abandon the research. But she persisted, and it is only within the past decade that her work has been confirmed.

Researchers have now seen signs of this kind of paternal inheritance in a number of recent studies. Some of the most interesting findings come from what is now an isolated resort community in northern Sweden called Överkalix parish, with mountains lit by the midnight sun in summer and the northern lights in winter.

Swedish researchers were drawn to Överkalix because careful historical records had been kept by town officials during the nineteenth century, when Överkalix was subject to repeated crop failures. Harvest statistics were collected in "Communications from the County Governor in Västerbotten to His Majesty the King," and grain prices were recorded as well. Researchers had information on children born in Överkalix in 1905, as well as data on bountiful harvests and starvation back to the time of the children's grandparents. The idea was to look for any connection between the grandparents' diets and the outcomes of their grandchildren. During bountiful years, the grandparents would have had plenty to eat, and during lean years they would not have had nearly enough. The scientists didn't know what they would find, but the data gave them the opportunity to see whether changes in men's nutrition could have any health consequences for their grandchildren.

They looked at records that would tell them about the diets of grandfathers during their early adolescent years, a period thought to be particularly important for future health.

And they found that diet at that stage of life had important consequences. The grandchildren of men who had plenty to eat did not live as long as those whose grandfathers had gone hungry. The grandfathers' hunger was good for grandchildren in other ways, too. The grandchildren of these men were less likely to die of heart disease or diabetes than those whose grandfathers had had plenty to eat as adolescents.

Marcus Pembrey of University College London has reviewed the Överkalix findings and other sources of information to see what else he could learn about men's behavior and diet and their effects on their children and grandchildren. He looked at data on 166 British fathers who said they'd started smoking before the age of eleven and compared their children to those of fathers who started smoking later in life. The sons of the fathers who started smoking early were more likely to be overweight by age nine. There seemed to be a link between fathers and their sons but not between fathers and their daughters.

Pembrey and his colleagues also looked again at the historical records of harvests in Överkalix to determine which grandparents had good access to nutrition in early adolescence and which did not. They confirmed the increased mortality risk in the grandsons of paternal grandfathers who had good access to food. And they found the same thing in granddaughters whose paternal grandmothers had plenty to eat. The opposite case was also true: grandchildren had lower mortality risk if their paternal grandparents had poor access to food as children.

There's more. We have known that mothers who overeat or are obese during pregnancy increase the chances that their children will be obese. And now we know that a similar thing happens with fathers. The children of obese mothers *and* fathers are more likely to be obese themselves. This result comes from Margaret J. Morris and her colleagues at the University of New South Wales in Australia. They noticed that overweight children usually had overweight mothers and fathers, and they wondered whether fathers' diets—not just their genes—would affect their children's risk of developing type 2 diabetes.

The researchers fed male rats of normal weight a diet of more than 40 percent fat, which made them obese. Then they mated them with females who had been fed a normal diet. The male pups showed increases in weight and body fat, and tests indicated they had an increased risk of diabetes. The daughters showed a different pattern. Their body fat and weight were normal when they were born, but in adulthood, they developed a diabetes-like condition marked by alterations in the way they handled glucose and insulin. When Morris and her team looked closely at the daughters' genes, they found alterations in the workings of 642 genes related to islet cells—the cells that produce insulin. There was only one explanation for this link: the fathers' high-fat diets had produced alterations in their sperm, which then led to the occurrence of adult-onset disease in their daughters.

These alterations are referred to as epigenetic changes. They do not change the DNA sequence of genes, but they affect whether or not certain genes are expressed—meaning whether they are turned on or off. The findings of the Överkalix and obesity studies reflect such epigenetic changes.

Other studies have shown a similar connection in other ailments. A group at the University of Massachusetts led by Oliver J. Rando found that feeding male mice a diet low in protein substantially altered many genes involved in the metabolism of cholesterol and fats in their offspring. The group offered some interesting speculation about why this might be the case. Perhaps the father's body, detecting that it is in an environment in which protein is in short supply, is altering the genes it passes on to its children to help them adapt to scarcity. "Mechanisms exist that could allow organisms to 'inform' their progeny about prevailing environmental conditions," the researchers wrote. That is a remarkable and unexpected way for a father to help ensure the survival of his offspring.

Each of these findings led to more research, and the evidence that poor health in fathers can adversely affect their children is mounting. In a more recent finding, Eric J. Nestler of the Mount Sinai School of Medicine in New York and his colleagues exposed adult male mice to chronic stress, and then bred them with normal females. The pups showed physiological and behavioral changes resembling those of depression and anxiety. Lorena Saavedra-Rodríguez and Larry A. Feig at Tufts University School of Medicine in Boston found that female mice passed the effects of stress on to their offspring, but fathers passed those effects on to their offspring and to the next generation as well—another example of the grandfather effect found in the Överkalix studies.

Studies such as these are appearing all the time. The more that researchers look for these changes, the more they find them. In a study presented at the annual meeting of the Society for Neuroscience in November 2013 and later published in *Nature*, Brian G. Dias and Kerry J. Ressler of Emory University in Atlanta reported that the fear produced by traumatic experiences can be passed on from males to their offspring. They gave male mice small shocks when the mice were exposed to a certain odor, until the mice would show a startle response when exposed to that particular odor, not to others. When the mice were mated, Dias and Ressler found that the offspring showed an increased startle response to the same odor. And this fear was passed on to the next generation, too.

It's important to remember that until the past decade, researchers did not anticipate finding anything like these epigenetic changes in fathers. It's not surprising that the health of mothers would affect their unborn children; a mother and her fetus have a very intimate connection. But the only connection between fathers and the fetus is the single sperm that fertilizes the egg. It carries within a rich, and sometimes harmful, legacy. The question that remains is how these experiences of the fathers manage to change the epigenetic marks on their sperm so that the health risks or fears of the fathers are passed on to their offspring. Researchers have only hypotheses; nobody knows for sure.

Other researchers have looked at the threats to fathers from toxins and pollution, to see whether exposure to these substances can produce changes in their offspring. Can toxins alter the operation of fathers' genes the way stress, diet, and anxiety can? The first studies to address this question were done by Michael K. Skinner, a biochemist at Washington State University. He began by exposing lab rats to a fungicide called vinclozolin, used in vineyards and on fruits and vegetables. He wouldn't have been surprised to find that exposure to the chemical harmed the rats. But he found much more than that. The fungicide switched on genes in the rats that normally were switched off, and vice versa—

and these changes in the operation of the genes were passed on to their offspring. Researchers have known for a long time that chemicals in the environment can alter the operation of genes. But they thought that the genes in sperm and eggs were scrubbed clean of these changes before being passed along at conception. Skinner found that this was not the case. It was quite the opposite—the alterations had become permanent. The flipped switches were passed on to the next generation.

If exposures to the environment could alter the workings of genes that were once thought to be protected from outside influences, then it made sense to see whether men's exposures to potentially toxic substances at work could produce harmful alterations in the operation of their genes. Tania A. Desrosiers and colleagues at the University of North Carolina did an epidemiological study in which they looked at large populations of male workers to see whether some jobs were associated with health problems in the men's children. The hypothesis proved to be correct. Certain occupations of fathers were associated with a greater risk of birth defects in their kids. The riskier occupations included petroleum or gas worker, chemical worker, printer, computer scientist, hairdresser, and motor vehicle operator. Certain jobs were associated with particular birth defects: cataracts and glaucoma were linked to photographers, while digestive abnormalities were linked to landscapers. Epidemiological studies such as this always require confirmation in the lab and clinic, so we can't yet be sure that this finding is correct. But it's an important warning sign.

•

These studies represent one unexpected way that fathers and even grandfathers can affect the health of their descendants. But there are other ways to look for connections between fathers and children's health. One way is to see whether any other paternal attributes contribute to health outcomes in children. Some researchers are trying to find out whether a man's looks have any consequences for his children. And they are finding provocative answers in, of all animals, zebra finches.

These birds, native to Australia, are about four inches long. The males have orange cheeks, striped gray-and-white throats, and red beaks. They might seem an unlikely species in which to pursue questions concerning men's attractiveness. How, for example, would an investigator distinguish a particularly handsome finch from his plainer counterparts? Yet finches have taught us something interesting about fatherhood: the handsomeness of a male makes a difference to his children.

I heard this story from James P. Curley of Columbia University, an authority on the genetics of fatherhood. He doesn't work on finches. He works on mice, which are also quite useful in the study of male genetics. But when I went to see him, he told me about the finches and walked me down the hall from his lab to a small room where some of his colleagues kept a noisy population of chattering zebra finches. Genetic tests of these small birds have shown that males can make important contributions to their offspring through an indirect route: by altering mothers' behavior. Male finches can help their offspring's chances of survival by making females become more adept at caring for their young.

The scientists who work with the finches looked at the

question of whether the attractiveness of a male affects a female's parenting behavior. The experiment was prompted by the curious sexual preferences of female finches, which have demonstrated that they prefer males wearing a red leg ring over males without one. The females show little interest in males with green leg bands. This discovery saved the researchers from having to figure out which finches are the best-looking. It turns out to be a question of choosing the proper accessories.

It's impossible to know for certain why the females prefer males adorned with red rings, but female zebra finches find males with big red cheek patches extremely attractive, Curley said, and the red rings could somehow be mimicking the cheek patches. Even without a firm explanation, this was a phenomenon the researchers could use to their advantage. They put red leg bands on half a group of male finches and green leg bands on the other half. Then they compared the offspring of the attractive males to those of the homely green-banded males.

The offspring of the attractive red-banded males were found to have distinct advantages. They begged for food more often than the others and were rewarded: mothers gave them more food. Females laid eggs containing more growth hormones when the eggs had been fertilized by the attractive males. You might guess that the attractive fathers simply had better genes, but that wasn't the case. Somehow, making the male finches more attractive encouraged mothers to devote more resources to the offspring. The attractive males didn't have better genes than their green-ringed competitors, although the females might have been tricked into thinking that they did.

Curley called the findings so unexpected as to seem

ridiculous. How could a colored leg band have such an important effect on mothers' behavior? He decided to see whether he could replicate the experiment with his mice, comparing males raised in isolation to "enriched males" raised in a more natural environment. Then he mated each one with a female. The females who mated with the enriched males devoted more resources to their offspring and engaged in more thorough maternal behavior. It was similar to what was going on with the finches—females invested more in their offspring when they had a more desirable mate.

Encouraged, Curley did another test, this one with stressed and normal males. Females who mated with normal males nursed and licked their offspring more often, and their pups exhibited less anxiety than the offspring of the stressed males. It was yet another demonstration of the same effect: making the males more desirable turned the females into better mothers. And that was good for their pups.

Continuing along these lines, Curley looked at whether a male's anxiety could affect his pups in the same way that stress did. To produce high-anxiety males, he took males out of their cages and dropped them into unfamiliar enclosures. Those who were the least willing to explore their new surroundings were the mice with the highest anxiety. He bred these males with females and found that the daughters of the high-anxiety fathers exhibited similar symptoms. The pups were raised solely by their mothers. The researchers concluded that marks on the fathers' sperm were being passed on to affect daughters' behavior, independent of any change in mothers' behavior. (These marks are referred to as epigenetic changes, because they change the operation

of genes—whether they are turned on or off—without actually changing the DNA.) And the sons did not inherit
their fathers' anxiety. This, too, parallels other findings. The
nutritional status of the Överkalix grandfathers affected
only their sons, not their daughters. It's clear that some of
these effects apply only to sons and others only to daughters.
The inability to explain this is a sign of how much more
researchers need to find out about these odd generational
effects.

Curley and his colleagues are now exploring a gene called
Peg3 that likewise has different effects on sons and daughters. The name stands for "paternally expressed genes": in
this family of genes only the father's copy is expressed in his
offspring, while the copy from mothers is silenced. "That
means what your father passes on to you is of massive significance," Curley said. He is studying the gene in mice, but
a form of *Peg3* occurs in humans, too. So anything he dis-
covers in his mice is likely to be true in us as well. To help
me understand what the gene does, Curley started with a
short lecture on mouse sex. Virgin male mice, he explained,
begin with a trial-and-error mating strategy: they pursue
any female they can, whether or not the female is in estrus,
ready to reproduce. The males usually manage to mate, and
then their troubles are over. Once they've mated, they
develop the ability to detect, by smell, which females are
in estrus. Curley wanted to know how *Peg3* might be involved in this behavior, and so he used a lab trick to inacti-
vate, or "knock out," the *Peg3* gene in some of his mice. The
knockout mice were unable to detect when females were
in estrus, even after they'd mated. They continued to try
mating with females who were not ready to reproduce. After a while, the directionless males gave up. So now Curley

knew that *Peg3* is essential for the development of proper behavior regarding sex and mating in males.

Curley then looked at females. There he discovered that knocking out *Peg3* had a very different effect. Knocking out *Peg3* in female mice doesn't affect mating, the way it does in males. Instead, females whose *Peg3* gene is knocked out become poor caretakers. They don't eat as much as they should early in their pregnancies. After birth, they are supposed to lick their pups, nurse them, eat the placenta (a source of nourishment), and build a nest. Females whose *Peg3* has been knocked out do those things much less frequently than normal mice.

To sum all this up, *Peg3* affects how well a father's male pups will mate and how well his female pups will care for their offspring. The mating ability of his sons and the nurturing qualities of his daughters will both affect the health of his grandpups. Once again, we have an effect that extends from males not only to their children but also to their grandchildren. It's reasonable to expect that the human version of *Peg3* has similar effects in human males and their offspring. That's not the same as proving the connection, but it gives Curley and others confidence to look for a similar phenomenon in humans.

We can't put people in cages, tag them with colorful jewelry, and allow them to mate. Unlike finches, who had no say in which leg band they got, human males might object to being made unattractive for the sake of an experiment. Nor would they appreciate being manipulated in a way that could harm their children. But mice, finches, and humans are enough alike that's what true in them is often true in us. Even though these findings haven't been confirmed in humans, it might be wise for men who are about to become fathers to think about their health and about what they should be eating even before their wives or partners become pregnant. This would be good advice for fathers even if it doesn't have any beneficial effects on their children. And it would be an even better idea if it does.

TWO

Conception:
The Genetic Tug-of-War

Years ago, when I had just started work as a science reporter at the Associated Press, I happened to get into a cab with a biology student from MIT. We were both on the way to a conference on cancer in Houston, and he was nervously preparing to make one of his first scientific presentations at a national meeting—on a study of the Y chromosome, the vehicle for fathers' genetic contributions to their kids. Our paths have crossed several times over the years, and I've watched his career soar. That student, David C. Page, is now the director of the distinguished Whitehead Institute for Biomedical Research in Cambridge, Massachusetts, affiliated with MIT. And he's still pursuing the questions he was interested in when we shared that cab.

He recently published a fascinating analysis of the history of the Y chromosome. It is, of course, essential for sexual reproduction. Males have one X chromosome and one Y; females have two Xs. Mothers pass one or the other of their Xs to each child; fathers pass an X, which makes the child a girl, or a Y, which makes it a boy. Page and his team showed that the Y chromosome, which is much smaller than the X when seen under a microscope, is only a fragmentary remnant of what it once was. At one point, the X and Y chromosomes had about eight hundred genes in common. The Y has now lost all but nineteen of those genes.

Are males disappearing?

Not quite: the *genes* have been disappearing, but males themselves are not withering away. Most of the gene loss occurred a long time ago, and the Y now seems to have stabilized. It's a lucky thing for fathers and for us: new research on the Y chromosome leads us on a fascinating tale of male genetics, which is far more complicated and important than you might expect, despite the loss of all those genes.

Until recently, we thought we had a pretty good understanding of how conception worked. Fathers and mothers each contribute 23 chromosomes to a fertilized egg, giving it the full complement of 46. (They all occur in matched pairs except the X and Y.) The fertilized egg then begins to divide into many kinds of cells, and ultimately grows into a fetus sharing traits from both its mother and its father. It seems simple enough. But as scientists developed the tools to fertilize eggs in the laboratory and study the process in greater detail, they discovered a much more interesting story.

In the late 1970s, M. Azim Surani was a young developmental biologist in Cambridge, England, in the laboratory of the physiologist Robert G. Edwards—better known as half of the team of Steptoe and Edwards, who developed in vitro fertilization, or IVF. Edwards and gynecologist Patrick C. Steptoe were responsible for the 1978 birth of the world's first so-called test-tube baby, Louise Brown, an achievement that would later be recognized with a Nobel Prize. Surani found the lab an enormously exciting place to be. The research on IVF was moving quickly when Surani joined the team, and Edwards wanted Surani to get involved in it. But Surani had a different idea.

He was interested in the phenomenon known as parthenogenesis, which gets its name from the Greek words for virgin birth. It's a form of reproduction in which healthy offspring arise from only a mother's genes or only a father's genes—not from a mix of the two, as is the case in sexual reproduction. Scientists knew at the time that it could occur in some fish, reptiles, and other animals. But it was not known to occur in mammals, including humans or laboratory mice. Surani wanted to see if he could manipulate mice in the lab to force a virgin birth.

In mice and humans, the sperm and the egg each contribute one set of chromosomes to a fertilized egg, which then has a pair of them. That's what it needs to divide and diversify. Combining two sets of a mother's genes in an egg would theoretically accomplish the same thing: it would give the egg the correct number of chromosomes. Everything that was then known about genetics suggested that such an egg, even though all its genes came from females, should develop normally.

By the time he left the Edwards lab, Surani and his assistant Sheila C. Barton had developed the tools he would need to manipulate genes and eggs. He used those tools to "fertilize" a mouse egg by inserting a copy of genes from another female. It didn't work. He tried the experiment repeatedly and failed each time. The eggs with only mothers' genes developed into tiny, fragile fetuses, but none of them survived. Shortly after they were implanted into foster mouse mothers, they died, riddled with genetic defects. Some grew more slowly and were smaller than normal embryos;

others had abnormally large yolk sacs. One had poorly organized brain tissue. Another had a beating heart, but no
head.

It was clear that fathers contributed something essential to the survival of developing embryos. No one had any
idea what that essential contribution was, but Surani was
determined to find out. Surani tried reversing the experiment: he produced fertilized eggs with two sets of fathers'
genes. Those embryos did not survive either. He knew his
experimental technique was correct, because when he
used the same equipment to combine fathers' genes with
mothers' genes, the embryos survived. His conclusion was
that mothers and fathers each contributed something with
their genes that marked them as "paternal" or "maternal"—
and that both were essential to the survival of the fertilized egg.

He knew that "something" wasn't in the genetic code
itself, which is the same for mothers' and fathers' genes. A
maternal hemoglobin gene is essentially indistinguishable
from a paternal hemoglobin gene (although there are minor
individual variations). The genes had to be marked in some
way that didn't alter the code. This was unexpected and difficult to accept at first. But it was an important new genetic
phenomenon. The principal reason that Surani's colleagues
didn't believe the finding was that the discovery violated
the genetic principles known as Mendel's laws, discovered
by the German monk Gregor Mendel in the mid-nineteenth
century. His work—which was lost for more than three
decades before being rediscovered in 1900—forms the
bedrock upon which modern genetics was built. Mendel
painstakingly bred pea plants for eight years to see how
different traits were passed from one generation to the

next. He bred tall plants with short plants, green peas with yellow peas, and so on, to see what would emerge in the offspring. The results were entirely unexpected and groundbreaking.

Before Mendel, biologists thought that crossing two different plants would produce something of a mix: crossing a plant with wrinkled seeds with another that had smooth seeds would produce plants with slightly wrinkled seeds. But that wasn't the case. Some plants had smooth seeds, and some had wrinkled seeds, depending on which way Mendel crossbred the plants. There *was* no in-between. These characteristics arrived in the next generation as discrete traits; they did not blend with each other. The traits were associated with genes that are passed from each parent to offspring and that do not blend with each other. Mendel could not know that; genes had not yet been discovered. He knew only what he saw in his pea plants.

To Mendel, whether a trait came from a mother or father made no difference. Genes combined in certain predictable ways no matter where they originated. Surani's work posed a direct challenge to this principle. Scientists had to decide whom they were going to believe—Mendel or Surani. That was no contest. Most scientists concluded that if Surani's work violated Mendel's principles, Surani was wrong. "Around 1983, people in Cambridge were starting to hear about these strange experiments, and I was invited to give a seminar in the department of genetics. I could see they were very skeptical," he recalled. "But I was convinced." He soon got some help from another researcher in the United States—Davor Solter, then at the Wistar Institute, an independent biomedical research center in Philadelphia. It so happened that Solter had been doing similar experiments, and he was coming up with the same findings. This was crucial: controversial results such as these are harder to dismiss when they're found independently in more than one laboratory.

In one of his early publications, Surani called these maternally or paternally marked genes "imprinted genes," as if they were stamped with an identifier saying they came from mother or father. The name stuck. Further research showed that most human genes are *not* imprinted. Only about 100 of the estimated 20,000 human genes have so far been found to carry these special chemical imprints, although some researchers believe there are more.

But what function do they serve? Surani examined all the mouse fetuses that failed to survive gestation. He saw that when he conducted the experiment with two sets of mothers' genes, the embryos developed reasonably well, but not the placentas. With paternal genes, the opposite was true: the placentas looked normal, but the embryos didn't develop properly. This was the first hint concerning what imprinted genes do. It didn't tell Surani much, but it did tell him that paternal genes and maternal genes were doing different things. Something about the imprinted genes of fathers was important for the development of the placenta, and the imprinted genes of mothers were important for the development of the embryo.

Evidence for imprinted genes continued to accumulate, and Surani and Solter eventually convinced their colleagues that the findings were legitimate. The existence of imprinted genes in humans was confirmed as well. Mendel wasn't wrong, exactly; his findings were merely incomplete. Even though only a small number of human genes are imprinted, that's enough to explain why parthenogenesis didn't work.

Offspring need one set of paternally imprinted genes and one set of maternally imprinted genes to survive.

Once geneticists recognized that imprinting was essential for reproduction, they realized that it can also make us vulnerable to a variety of severe genetic disorders. In the case of genes that aren't imprinted, we have an insurance policy. We get one copy from each parent, and the two are interchangeable. If one fails, the other often keeps working, and so we stay healthy. There's a good reason that evolution endowed us with backup copies of most genes. Mutations are fairly common, and so illness and malfunctions would be much more common if we were not able to switch to an un damaged backup that can function like an emergency power supply in a blackout. It usually doesn't matter which version of a gene works, as long as one of them does. But with imprinted genes, one copy is stamped "off." That's why imprinting has such a huge cost. If a mutation occurs in the single working copy, we're in trouble. You might expect that such mutations would be devastating, and that is precisely what scientists have found.

I found Surani's groundbreaking work fascinating. Here was a critically important way in which fathers contributed to their children's well-being that was important to scientists and also to families who have children with these illnesses. I've written about genetics and inherited diseases often enough to know that we all walk a very thin line between health and disease. A single stutter or typo in the genetic code can mean the difference between a healthy child and one who is very sick or who does not survive. With the discovery of imprinting, it now seemed that line was even thinner and more perilous. I decided I should talk to children with some of these illnesses, and their parents, to show that what might seem like an abstract finding in genetics can have serious consequences for fathers and their children.

My first visit was with the family of Alexander Baker on Manhattan's Upper West Side. Alexander, a bright, cheery, and exceedingly friendly child, was about to turn five. When I walked in, he was deeply involved in a game on his iPad but pleased to have a visitor in the house. He looked up and greeted me with a broad smile before turning back to his iPad, but kept stealing glances at me while I talked to his parents. Alexander's mother, Maria, thirty-five, is a writer, and his father, Thomas, also thirty-five, is an HR director. Their second child, James, nearly a year old, rested quietly in Maria's arms.

When I opened my laptop to take notes on our conversation, Alexander immediately ran behind me to look over my shoulder and see what I was doing. When I showed him, he smiled, nodded, and watched for a while before returning to his iPad. (Sociability is a characteristic of children with Angelman syndrome.) After I'd been there about twenty minutes, he handed the tablet to Maria and pointed at something on the screen. She looked at him and said, "Say 'Help me.'" He hesitated and then said it. The phrase is one of only a few that he can manage to say. He learned them through extensive drills with a speech therapist. In addition to being unable to speak, Alexander is developmentally delayed, has frequent seizures, and will require care for the rest of his life.

Thomas and Maria suspected something was going on with Alexander in the first few months of his life. By the time he was eight months old, when he was diagnosed with multiple developmental delays, they were certain. "We were very aware of signs of trouble," Thomas told me. "People around us would say that we were new parents and we worried too much—and that boys were slower to develop." But they knew that wasn't it. They began making the rounds with various specialists, eventually seeing more than twenty of them—geneticists, developmental pediatricians, and neurologists. "These were possibly the hardest and most painful years in our lives so far—knowing that there was something wrong and going into appointment after appointment, and coming out with no answers or another misdiagnosis."

Diagnoses of autism and cerebral palsy were suggested but soon rejected. Doctors then concluded that he had what they call pervasive developmental delay (PDD), which sounds official but is merely a blanket diagnosis that means he was failing to meet the usual infant and child milestones for development. Because they had no idea what caused it, they labeled it PDD "not otherwise specified," or PDD-NOS.

The Bakers shared the news with their families and then got their first break. Thomas's brother-in-law's sister called. She had written a research paper on Angelman syndrome for a college biology class, and she immediately thought of Alexander. His lack of speech and the way he flapped his hands when he was excited sounded to her like it could be Angelman. Those can be signs of autism, too, so she couldn't be sure, but it was another lead. Alexander's parents went back to the experts, who quickly dismissed the concern. But they persisted. In November 2008, just before Thanksgiving, Alexander was tested, and the diagnosis of Angelman syndrome was confirmed. "It was a bittersweet moment," Maria told me. It was a relief to find out what was wrong. But they now knew they were dealing with a very serious condition that couldn't be easily corrected. "Before that," Thomas said, "we hoped it was a phase he could outgrow." The Bakers quickly learned that Angelman syndrome is a rare and severe disorder of the nervous system. There is no treatment for it, although parents of children with Angelman syndrome have identified a long list of therapies that they think and hope will ease the symptoms. Thomas and Maria told me that Alexander gets "every type of therapy you might imagine." These include attending a special therapeutic school; occupational therapy to tune his fine-motor skills; a kind of physical therapy intended to improve balance and movement called the Feldenkrais Method; speech therapy; aquatherapy; and, every weekend, special therapy on horseback intended to move his hips in a way that will help him walk better. Some of this is covered by insurance, but a lot of it is not. Maria has put her career on hold while she works full-time as a caretaker for Alexander.

While it's common for children with Angelman syndrome to have seizures, the form those seizures take can change. Not long ago, Alexander entered a period in which he seemed distant and unable to respond. The Bakers didn't know what to make of it at first, but his doctors determined that he was having what are called nonconvulsive seizures. By the time he was diagnosed, he had gone through a month of almost continuous seizures; that's what had led to the vacant look. Seizures are not only dangerous in themselves, but they lead to setbacks in Alexander's other treatments.

In the absence of a cure, Alexander will need intensive

care for a lifetime. He is a charming child, but there are developmental milestones that he will likely never achieve. He still wears a diaper at night and will probably never be able to dispense with it. And while the Bakers have a warm and loving relationship with Alexander, which he reciprocates, they know their lives together will be difficult, as Thomas explained. "We are never likely to have him tell us that he loves us—at least in those words. We will continue to need to guess at whether he had a good day or a bad day, or if something hurts. We worry about what our lives will look like when our adorable young boy becomes a teenager or young adult, and his drool and need to hug everyone he sees won't be as cute or as welcome by others." The Bakers have struggled to provide as much care for Alexander as they could afford. In the meantime, they wait and desperately hope for a cure, or anything that might improve Alexander's outlook.

All of Alexander's symptoms are due to a mutation in a cluster of imprinted genes on human chromosome number 15. These are maternally imprinted genes, meaning they are operational only when inherited from a mother—the technical term is that they are maternally expressed. The copy children inherit from their fathers is turned off in the brain. When the mother's copy isn't present or isn't functioning because of some error or abnormality in the gene, the child has no working copy. The silent copy from the father can't serve as a backup to remedy the lack of this critical gene.

But that's not the end of the story. The cluster of genes on chromosome 15 that cause Angelman syndrome also contains a gene that is expressed only when it comes from the *father*. When this paternal gene is not expressed, children are born with a disorder called Prader-Willi syndrome.

These children have developmental delays similar to those seen in Angelman syndrome. But one hallmark of Prader-Willi is its curious effect on eating. Children with the syndrome don't nurse well and are generally underweight before weaning. After weaning, however, the children develop voracious appetites and almost inevitably become obese. They also show developmental and physical delays, including poor muscle tone, which can affect their movement. As with Angelman, there are a variety of therapies that can ease some symptoms, but there is no treatment that comes even close to a cure.

Prader-Willi represents a different example of the failure of imprinted genes. It is caused by a mutation in the same cluster of genes that cause Angelman syndrome, but in this case it's a paternally imprinted gene that is afflicted with a mutation. After my visit with the Bakers, I got in touch with the family of a boy with Prader-Willi syndrome. We arranged for a visit, and one night shortly afterward I took the Long Island Rail Road from Manhattan to the home of Michael Stevens, thirty-eight, an accountant in New York City. His son, James, was five and in kindergarten. He and his wife, Barbara, thirty-seven, a nurse, were not unlike the Bakers. Both families had the means to provide extra help to their children, including therapies not covered by insurance. Barbara, like Maria, had stopped working outside the home to become James's full-time caretaker.

Michael and Barbara were fortunate to get a proper diagnosis for James shortly after he was born. Signs of trouble had appeared late in the pregnancy, when doctors noted unusually low fetal movement. Their doctor decided to induce the birth early, in case there was a problem. When James was born, he didn't cry. Barbara had developed gestational diabetes, and because that can cause the fetus to gain weight, James was sent to the intensive-care unit for observation. The specialist there suspected Prader-Willi syndrome. James's testicles had not descended—a key indicator. And Barbara was zeroing in on that diagnosis, too; as a pediatric therapist, she had worked with children with Prader-Willi. "I didn't even get to fire up the cigar, you know?" Michael said. Genetic tests confirmed the diagnosis two weeks later. James was in the hospital for six weeks.

Barbara was feeding James dinner when Michael and I arrived at their house. Because of the danger of overeating and obesity, Barbara feeds James and controls his diet rigorously. He eats four times a day—200 calories for breakfast, 300 for lunch, 200 at afternoon snack time, and 300 for dinner. Barbara also gives him human growth hormone, fish oil, coenzyme Q10 supplements, an amino acid supplement, carnitine, calcium, multivitamins, and a laxative, the last because of digestive problems associated with the disorder. He hasn't yet developed the insatiable appetite, but they know the day is coming. "This is the fearsome, daunting characteristic of the syndrome that people dread," Michael said. "You hear stories of teenagers who are 400 pounds."

Although Prader-Willi children are not known for the sociability that is seen in Angelman syndrome, I found James to be just as charming as Alexander. Like Alexander, he seemed happy to have a visitor. When his mother and I went upstairs to see his bedroom, he ran up behind us, wanting to show it to me himself. He was especially proud of his electric guitar, which he was just learning to play. James's intelligence is "at the low end of normal," Barbara said.

When James was born, Barbara and Michael were ready to buy a new house, and they took James's special needs into consideration. The house they built has a kitchen and pantry that can be completely sealed off from the rest of the house. The cabinets and doors are locked. "Kids are up in the middle of the night, grabbing food, stealing food, eating out of the trash—I can't tell you how many stories we hear like that," Barbara said. "If they know they can't get at it, it's better for them." This is not just hearsay; extreme and insatiable appetite is a hallmark of Prader-Willi syndrome.

My visits with Alexander and James and their parents helped me understand the consequences of disorders in imprinted genes, and the seriousness of the boys' illnesses underscored how important imprinting is. While mothers and fathers both make genetic contributions to their children, this was another area of research in which it was clear that the contributions of fathers extend far beyond what you might expect from the tiny package of DNA carried inside a single sperm.

Genes that can lead to such serious illnesses would not have arisen in evolutionary history if there wasn't a very important reason for them to be there. After my visits with Alexander and James, I looked for someone who could explain why imprinting occurs to begin with and what it might tell us about what fathers contribute to their children. That led me to David Haig at Harvard.

A few years after Surani's discovery of imprinting, Haig, then a young biologist in Australia, was preparing for a career that would one day lead him to a fascinating explanation for why imprinting exists. Now a professor of evolutionary biology, Haig almost abandoned the field after his college graduation for a life of travel and adventure. Instead, he decided to work toward a Ph.D. in what seemed to be an obscure corner of evolutionary biology: conflict between parents and offspring in plants. But the work he did then would ultimately help him develop what he calls "the kinship theory" to explain why genetic imprinting occurs.

To get to Haig's office in Harvard's Museum of Comparative Zoology, visitors must walk through the museum exhibits and past the famous Blaschka glass flowers. Haig has no laboratory. His job is not to do experiments, but to try to explain the results of others' lab work. His greatest experimental achievement, early in his career, involved counting "a quarter of a million bristles on fly bellies," he said, and that was enough to drive him out of the laboratory for good.

As his research led him beyond the study of plants, Haig began to explore the curious competition that occurs between parents and their offspring. In 1993, Haig published a paper on one aspect of the competition—a conflict that occurs between the mother and the fetus during pregnancy. Fathers might have reasons to compete with mothers, too, but Haig showed that a fetus does so even while utterly dependent upon her for survival. "Pregnancy has commonly been viewed as a cooperative interaction between a mother and her fetus," he wrote. But that's not true. It's warfare in which "fetal actions are opposed by maternal countermeasures."

One rather remarkable example of this is the ability of the fetus to alter its mother's arteries so they can't constrict. The fetus can then harvest whatever nutrients it wants from the mother's bloodstream, through the placenta. And she is powerless to resist. That control also means that the fetus can release hormones directly into the mother's bloodstream. One such hormone alters the mother's regulation of insulin. The fetus can make its mother's blood sugar rise. As that sugar-rich blood circulates through the placenta, it delivers more sugar to the fetus. But if the process goes too far—if the mother loses too much control over her blood sugar—the mother can develop diabetes, as was the case with James's mom, Barbara. According to Haig, gestational diabetes is just one possible outcome of the survival struggle between mother and fetus.

Other hormones are believed to increase the mother's blood pressure, enhancing the flow of blood to the fetus. If these fetal hormones overwhelm the mother, she can develop dangerously high blood pressure. This, too, is seen in the clinic. The condition is called preeclampsia, and when it occurs, blood pressure can climb to a level at which it becomes fatal. Haig marvels at these delicate relationships. "Natural selection produces things on this planet that are much more complex than any nonliving part of the universe. I come out of evolutionary biology, and I'm wanting to address this question—why has this thing evolved?"

As he was trying to work that out, he began thinking about another kind of genetic conflict, not between parent and child, but between parent and parent. It was an outgrowth of the work of Surani and Solter and others. He knew that they had found there was something that differentiated mothers' genes from fathers' genes. Haig was trying to explain why that is the case.

The result was his kinship theory. In broad terms, it goes something like this: Fathers and mothers both have strong interests in seeing their offspring survive. But they want different things for their children, because their reproductive strategies differ. In most mammals, the male is unlikely to mate with a given female more than once. He mates, moves on, and mates again. He doesn't care whether that leaves her too depleted to have further offspring. They're not his. Females, on the other hand, pursue the opposite strategy. Each of her young ties up a female for a good portion of her reproductive life. She is unable to mate as often and have as many children as a male, so she has to make sure that all her offspring survive. It's a case of quality over quantity. With any given pregnancy, her strategy is to give the embryo what it needs, but no more. That conserves her resources for her subsequent children. Expending too many resources on one offspring might leave her undersupplied for the next, risking its life or her own. The male, on the other hand, wants to extract as much of the mother's energy and resources as he can for *his* offspring. Or, as Haig puts it, "Maternal genes have a substantial interest in the mother's well-being and survival. Paternal genes favor greater allocation of maternal time and effort to their particular child."

The stage is now set for competition. The male and female do whatever they can to advance their competing strategies. But how do they do that? How can a father manipulate the mother to extract maximum resources for the child? And how can a mother conserve her resources and make sure that doesn't happen? Haig's insight was that imprinted genes are the weapons that males and females use to pursue their competing strategies. The imprints that mothers and fathers put on the genes turn them off or on as needed to pursue these strategies.

The gene's "imprint" is stamped on it by the parent, and that imprint affects the expression of the gene in the offspring.

The genes that are expressed when inherited from fathers tend to encourage more growth in the fetus. They push the fetus to demand more resources from its mother while it's in the womb—to suck up as many maternal resources as possible, pursuing the father's competitive strategy. Genes that are expressed when inherited from mothers tend to slow that growth, so the mother can conserve resources for subsequent children.

Haig's theory was meant to explain not only what Surani had found but also what others found as they began to explore the implications of Surani's research. While Surani can claim credit for discovering the phenomenon of imprinting, he didn't know which genes were imprinted or precisely what each of them did. It took about a decade for researchers to discover the first imprinted gene. That was the work of Elizabeth Robertson, then in the Department of Genetics and Development at Columbia University and now at the University of Oxford in England. She was investigating normal growth and development in mice by inactivating, or knocking out, certain genes to see what effect that would have on developing embryos. In a paper published in *Cell* in 1991, Robertson and her colleagues reported an unusual discovery regarding a gene called *Igf2*, which is responsible for the production of something called insulin-like growth factor II, or IGF-II. When the researchers knocked out the gene in mouse mothers, nothing happened. The offspring were normal. That meant the gene must have little or no role in the offspring's development. But when Robertson knocked it out in mouse *fathers*, the embryos grew to only about 60 percent of the size of their normal counterparts. When the gene came from a father—and only when it came from a father—it was clearly essential for growth.

This fit nicely with Haig's theory. The paternal gene enabled the fetus to draw more nutrients from its mother, a crucial part of the father's mating strategy. This was critical experimental evidence of the competition between mothers and fathers. Other researchers quickly followed with the discovery of other imprinted genes, and the genes that came from the fathers encouraged fetal growth, as Haig theorized. Taken to the extreme, this strategy had a serious drawback: if the fetus extracted too much from its mother, she would die, and so would the fetus.

The new discoveries also began to reveal mothers' powerful counterweapon: genes that are maternally stamped fight back against the male strategy, encouraging the fetus to draw only the nutrients it needs to survive, not as many as it can. Mothers put their stamp on a gene that counters the growth boost by *Igf2*. It's called *Igf2r*, and it's the gene for what's called the IGF-II receptor. In order for the male's IGF-II to work, it must plug into the IGF-II receptor. If the female controls the receptor, she can moderate the greedy nutrient-seeking of IGF-II. Denise P. Barlow and colleagues at the Research Institute of Molecular Pathology in Vienna discovered that Haig's theory held once again. *Igf2r*, as expected, was also imprinted—but in the opposite direction. The receptor gene was active only when it came from the mother. When the *Igf2r* gene is knocked out in fathers, nothing happens. But when the *Igf2r* gene is knocked out in female mice, the offspring grow too big and die before birth.

Haig published a paper about this fascinating competition with a title worthy of Sherlock Holmes: "Genomic

Imprinting and the Strange Case of the Insulin-like Growth Factor II Receptor." In it, Haig writes, with appropriate Sherlockian flourish, "Surely, it is no coincidence that IGF-II and its type 2 receptor are oppositely imprinted." For Haig, this was an exciting confirmation of his theory. The two genes enabled the parents to battle over the size of their offspring, each of them advancing his or her own evolutionary goals. To those who might be critical of his theory, Haig chose Holmes himself to respond: "It is an old maxim of mine that when you have excluded the impossible, whatever remains, however improbable, must be the truth."

Humans have counterparts to these genes, and when this system goes awry, the consequences can be devastating. Suppose, for example, a mother's and father's copies of *IGF2* (scientists capitalize the names of human genes and use lowercase letters to indicate nonhuman genes) are both mistakenly turned on—the mother's isn't turned off as it should be. Or suppose the fertilized egg accidentally gets two copies of the father's turned-on gene. The fetus then gets a double dose of growth genes. This leads to a condition called Beckwith-Wiedemann syndrome, in which children have birth weights more than 50 percent above normal. And the opposite mistake can occur. If both genes are silenced, the fetus doesn't draw on its mother's resources the way it should, and it is born below normal weight.

"It's a tug-of-war," Haig said. "You've got these two sides tugging on the rope. They're not shifting much—it's just a little bit one way or the other. And they come to depend on each other, on the other side holding the rope. If you get a mutation in an imprinted gene, you get a really pathological outcome. One side has let go of the rope."

Until recently, genes subject to this gender division were

thought to be rare, numbering perhaps a hundred or so out of the estimated 25,000 human genes. But Haig and his colleague Catherine Dulac, a Harvard molecular biologist, used a different method to find imprinted genes and concluded that there could be more than a thousand of them. Some critics have questioned this result, arguing that the study had flaws and that imprinted genes are not as common as Haig and Dulac claim. But whether or not that's the case, it's clear that this genomic battle of the sexes is not a rare phenomenon that plays out in isolated corners of the human genome—it's far more widespread.

Whatever the actual number of imprinted genes turns out to be, it is already clear that many of them are expressed only in the brain, where they can affect behavior in many ways. Indeed, maternal and paternal genes battle for control in the brains of every one of us. As Catherine Dulac told me, "We know we get conflicting advice from mom and dad. Here it's in the genome—it's in your own brain! So you can't escape mom and dad fighting over what you're supposed to do." But these imprinted genes are not expressed in all parts of the brain. That raises an interesting question. Research has shown that imprinting errors can affect a fetus's growth and even threaten its life. Could errors in imprinted *brain* genes be linked to mental illness?

Christopher Badcock of the London School of Economics and Bernard Crespi of Simon Fraser University in British Columbia think so. They believe that disruptions of the tug-of-war between imprinted genes in the brain could help to explain the origins of some mental illnesses—from autism to schizophrenia. This theory could also help to solve a long-standing riddle about the genetics of mental illness. Many of these illnesses tend to run in families, but it's not a question of simple inheritance, like eye color. Once again, the facts collide with Mendel's laws. Many of the inheritance patterns of mental illness are complex and poorly understood. They don't follow the usual rules. That suggests that imprinting errors might have something to do with these ailments. If so, an understanding of what's going on could lead to new treatments.

According to Crespi, there is already a link. Children with Beckwith-Wiedemann syndrome, the disorder of excessive growth associated with the $IGF2$ gene, have larger-than-normal brains and an increased risk of autism. Studies of people with autism—but without Beckwith-Wiedemann syndrome—have shown that they, too, can have larger-than-normal brains. "There is a good bit of evidence for overgrowth of the entire body and the brain in autism," Crespi says. "And there is work that has linked that to $IGF2$."

Crespi and Badcock then looked at the opposite situation—when a fetus lacks proper expression of the $IGF2$ genes and is smaller than normal. Would it have a condition that was somehow the "opposite" of autism? People with autism are unable to appreciate what is going on in groups of people around them. They have difficulty understanding what others are thinking. Now imagine individuals with an *enhanced* sensitivity to social cues, even to the point that they seem to "read into" others' behavior things that are not happening. Such people might hear voices that are not there—a hallmark of schizophrenia. Crespi and Badcock devised a spectrum of mental illnesses based on their possible connection with imprinting disorders. Autism is at one end of their spectrum, and schizophrenia, bipolar disorder, and depression are at the other end. Crespi and Badcock do not think that imprinting and their mental-illness spectrum explain everything about mental illness. But it is essential, they say, to find all the imprinted genes in the brain, discover what they do, and explore how variations in those genes might be related to psychiatric ailments.

Crespi also notes that recent findings fit his predictions. In people with schizophrenia, researchers have found reduced activity of three genes that are active when they come from fathers. According to Crespi, a reduction in expression of paternal genes should tip a person toward the schizophrenia-depression end of the spectrum. And that is what happens. Crespi believes that progress in understanding the connection between imprinting and mental illness is moving slowly because psychiatrists are generally not aware of the work of biologists studying imprinting, and vice versa.

This was an idea that occurred to me often while I was working on this book. Crespi is correct to say that psychiatrists and biologists don't talk to one an other nearly enough. But it's also true that psychologists don't talk to neuroscientists, evolutionary biologists don't talk to doctors, and epidemiologists don't talk to sociologists. The story of fathers and their children draws on all these scientific fields, but there is little cross-pollination among them.

"One of the things that hasn't been done in the field is to connect across levels," Crespi said. "You want to connect from the genetic level to the brain-structure level to the psychiatric level." His work with Badcock is a step in that direction: "It's bringing together two very different areas—social evolution theory connecting with psychiatry. I think I'm at least getting people to think more about evolutionary biology in the study of autism and schizophrenia." The field of psychiatry could use a good injection of evolutionary biology.

One of the reasons I find Haig's and Crespi's work so interesting is that it forces us to rethink what it means to be a human being. The traditional view was that an individual was "something that cannot be divided," but now the individual *is* divided. "If our genes disagree amongst themselves, I think the self is the arbiter among all these competing agendas," Haig told me. The body is not a machine. Instead, we're each organized "more like a social entity, with internal politics and agents with competing agendas." And this clashing of agendas inside us might even be something we can see. We hesitate over decisions. We decide whether to cooperate or compete, or waver between immediate gratification and long-term planning. Maybe what we're seeing and feeling in these situations is the settling of scores among our competing genes.

Alexander Baker's father Thomas, wrote to me after our visit. He was optimistic about new research that could point the way to a cure—or at least a partial cure—for Angelman syndrome. He was referring to work done by Benjamin Philpot and colleagues at the University of North Carolina. Researchers now know that Angelman syndrome is caused by the deletion or mutation of a maternal gene called *UBE3A*. As I've noted, the gene is expressed in the brain only if it's inherited from the mother. Fathers pass along a copy of the gene, too, but it is silenced in the child's brain. What if the father's copy could be turned on? Would it do the job of the missing maternal gene, and restore Alexander and others to something much closer to a normal life?

Philpot screened various chemical compounds, using neurons from mice, and he found a dozen that could activate the dormant paternal *Ube3a* gene as a backup to replace the mutated maternal copy. He also determined how the compounds worked. Next, he injected them into live mice, and he found that the paternal gene was activated in parts of the brain and spinal cord. And it remained active in spinal cord neurons for twelve weeks after he stopped administering the drug. Scientists are often reluctant to draw too many conclusions from animal research, so I was surprised to see that Philpot himself was also optimistic about the potential of his research. Philpot cautioned that drugs such as the ones he studied can have harmful effects elsewhere in the genes or the body, and it will take a while to sort that out before human trials can begin. If the drugs also affect the genes related to Prader-Willi syndrome, they could flip a child with Angelman to Prader-Willi, not a good outcome.

Nevertheless, this is an exciting development. One of the drugs Philpot studies is already approved for a kind of meningitis, which is a huge advantage. When the FDA approves a drug, doctors are generally free to prescribe it however they wish. That means that Philpot's drug can be legally prescribed to children with Angelman without years of studies to seek FDA approval. If Philpot is successful, the research could lead to similar treatments for other diseases of imprinting.

Nature has left us with these unusual genes that don't have working backup copies. But the backup copies are still there, and if researchers can find a way to turn them on safely, many of these diseases could be alleviated, or possibly cured. The discovery of imprinting and the theories to explain it show that fathers' genetic contributions to their children are far richer and more complex than we might have guessed. As we will see in the next chapter, the influence of fathers on their children continues during pregnancy. It's a time when fathers and their fetuses seem to have no discernible tie, but remain closely connected.

THREE

Pregnancy: Hormones, Depression, and the First Fight

If there was any point in a family's life when we'd think fathers don't matter much to children, it might be during pregnancy and infancy. It seems that biology has assigned the principal responsibilities to mothers during those months. But biology has a role for fathers to play during pregnancy, too. And it involves changes in their bodies, just as it does in those of their partners. The physical and psychological changes women undergo during pregnancy are paralleled by similar changes in their partners. And there is an important connection between fathers' behavior during pregnancy and their later involvement with their children: what happens to a father before his child's birth can affect the kind of father he will be for years to come.

Philip A. Cowan and his wife, Carolyn Pape Cowan, of the University of California, Berkeley, were among the first to study fathers during their partners' pregnancy. The study was prompted, in large part, by their own experience. They married young—Carolyn was nineteen and about to start her first full-time job as a teacher. Philip was twenty-one and still in college. They had both worked while in school as teenagers, so they felt equipped to able to enter the adult world, including getting married.

Two years after they married, they began trying to start a family. Carolyn was ready, but she admits that she pushed Philip. Their first daughter, Joanna, was born healthy, and so were their next two, Dena and Jonathan, born two and four years later. This was in the early 1960s, when most women stayed home to take care of the kids. Carolyn quit her teaching job and became a full-time mother.

When their first child was two and a second was on the way, they moved from Canada to California, where Philip had a new job. The stress of the move, away from family and friends, was far greater than they had anticipated. With Philip working and Carolyn at home, they began to feel more distant from each other. Differences and conflicts over parenting were driving them apart. It was, you might say, their first fight—their first real fight, with potentially grave consequences.

"We hadn't anticipated that having a baby could revive long-buried feelings of gratitude or disappointment about how loved we had felt as children, or realized that our disagreements about whether the baby needed to be picked up and comforted or left alone to 'cry it out' would actually have more to do with our own needs than they did with the baby's," they recalled in their book *When Partners Become Parents: The Big Life Change for Couples*. "Not only were we unprepared for these conflicts inside or between us but we found ourselves unable to talk about them productively once they surfaced," they reported. Their ten-year marriage was suddenly and unexpectedly in trouble.

They weren't the only ones struggling. Friends in similar circumstances were separating or divorcing all around them. Most of those couples had wanted to have children and had been excited at the prospect of starting a family. And yet the responsibilities of raising children, it seemed, were almost more than they could handle. "Almost all of us could trace the beginning of our difficulties back to those early years of becoming a family," Carolyn and Philip wrote. The phenomenon has been found in all kinds of families in multiple studies across the country and around the world. The Cowans and their friends couldn't understand it: What, they asked, is wrong with us?

As it happens, the Cowans had moved to California because Philip was offered a position as a psychologist at the University of California, Berkeley, where he ultimately became a professor of psychology. In the 1970s, prompted by curiosity and self-preservation, Philip began working with Carolyn, who had since become a psychologist, to prepare for what would be a fifteen-year study of ninety-six couples that would become a landmark in social science research— the Becoming a Family Project. Finally they would be able to investigate the reasons behind their own marital difficulties, as well as those of others.

The study included seventy-two couples expecting children and twenty-four similar couples without children. The Cowans followed them until the children reached their first year of elementary school. They also established couples groups, led by trained male-female teams, which met weekly for six months from before the babies' births until after. In these groups, partners discussed issues about their own well-being and mental health, their relationship as a couple, their ideas about what kind of parents they wanted to be, their intentions about what to carry over and what to discard from the families they grew up in, and how to deal with work and other stresses in their lives outside the family.

Among many other findings, the study had a lot to say about what happens to fathers during pregnancy. In the data they collected from their Becoming a Family Project, the Cowans found that during their partners' pregnancies, some men decided to grow beards, some lost weight, and some suddenly found themselves nursing injuries they hadn't noticed before. These were mostly exterior manifestations of inner change, it turned out. "As much as we pushed . . . for detail, though, talk about physical symptoms usually ended quickly, while talk about psychological and relationship changes could have gone on long into the night," they wrote.

In the lengthier conversations, some men reported internal emotional changes that could put their marriages at risk. These included difficulty talking with their wives about their emotions or their expectations of pregnancy and parenthood; changes in their sex lives; and unrealistic expectations about how they would share child care and housekeeping chores once the baby arrived. Most of the men in the Cowans' study seemed to think that there were rules they should follow, and those often included not saying they were vulnerable at a time when their wives needed them to be strong. But that posed a problem. When men think they should keep their worries hidden, they stop talking to their wives about things that matter to them. That was leading to increased tension and distance between the partners.

Some of the couples in the study blamed each other for their distress. One father-to-be found himself working longer hours as the pregnancy progressed, just when his wife wanted his help setting up the baby's room and otherwise preparing for the birth. She blamed him for making bad decisions in his business that now made the extra work necessary. Her criticism of his business decisions kept him at work even longer, because he wanted to show her that the business would succeed. He said that if she'd encouraged him in his work, he wouldn't have felt he had to work late every night.

Many men in the Cowans' study talked about doing things differently than their own fathers had. Most of them had grown up in traditional families in which the father was often away at work, and emotionally distant when he was home. "Almost every expectant father told us of his determination to have more of a presence with his sons and daughters than his father had with him," the Cowans wrote. One expectant father told them that his father "always felt so distant. I still have trouble talking to him about anything that matters. My children are going to know me and be able to talk to me about whatever's on their minds. They're not going to have any doubt about how I feel about them."

The Cowans' study, which ran from 1979 to 1990, was done at a time when women were not as likely to be working outside the home as they are now. Many men put more effort into their work, they told the Cowans, in anticipation of the increased financial responsibility they would soon have taking care of their wives and children. The expectant mothers often saw it differently—as a form of withdrawal.

Twenty percent of the couples the Cowans followed were divorced by the time their children reached kindergarten. But that didn't necessarily mean things were fine for the other 80 percent. Some of them had severe reservations about their marriages and were heading toward divorce. Philip worried about the conflict in those families and its effect on their children.

The Cowans did find some good news, and it had to do with fathers: the children of fathers who embraced and supported their partners' pregnancy had an easier transition years later, when they went to kindergarten. Happier couples, it almost goes without saying, provide more nurturing, and children who receive more nurturing enter school feeling loved and supported. And that can help them beyond kindergarten as well.

The Cowans noted that in most of their families, fathers of babies and young children did less of the family work at home than mothers did. But the future, they wrote, lies with men who are taking a more significant role in running the household and raising the children. "If we listen carefully to what those men and their wives are telling us, we can see that these men tend to feel better about themselves and about their family relationships than men who are less involved in family work. What's more, their wives feel significantly better too."

The changes that occur in men during pregnancy have been observed by many others as well, confirming the reports from the Cowans' families. During pregnancy, mothers experience a variety of profound hormonal and physical changes that help to prepare them for the substantial task of carrying and nurturing the fetus and new baby. That's not news; what *is* news is that men also undergo hormonal turmoil. One of the most obvious changes is the weight gain that many men experience along with their wives during pregnancy. Many women experience cravings and of course require more food during pregnancy. The men's weight gain could be occurring simply because they are tempted by all that extra food in the house. We don't need hormones to explain that. Anthropologists have discovered that this phenomenon, called couvade (from the French word meaning "to hatch"), occurs not only in Britain and the United States but in non-Western societies, too, "sometimes to an even more extreme and incapacitating degree," the Cowans write. In Papua New Guinea, some men, while waiting for their babies to be born, "retire to bed with unremitting nausea and incapacitating back problems, demand to be looked after, and otherwise raise an emotional fuss during the last months of their wives' pregnancies."

One of the key hormones that's affected is the sex hormone testosterone. And the other is prolactin, a hormone involved in the production of milk by nursing mothers. Men have prolactin, too, even though they don't nurse children. Why its levels should change in men has been a mystery. We've known that hormonal changes occurred in some animal species in which the fathers participated in rearing their offspring; prolactin levels rise in primates, in male birds just before they become parents, and in rodent species in which fathers help to care for their offspring. But nobody had shown much interest in looking at human fathers, to see whether something similar might be going on. In a paper published in 2000, Anne E. Storey, Katherine E. Wynne-Edwards, and their colleagues at Memorial University in Newfoundland began their study by acknowledging that lack of research: "Little is known about the physiological and behavioral changes that expectant fathers undergo prior to the birth of their babies," they wrote. Based on the findings in animals, Storey and company predicted they would find similar changes in male humans, beginning during their partners' pregnancy and continuing after birth. And they predicted that the variation in hormonal levels in any individual would be related to men's symptoms during pregnancy and their responsiveness to their infants.

They recruited thirty-four couples taking prenatal classes at a nearby hospital and took blood samples from the men before and after the births of their babies. All but three of the couples were first-time parents. The couples were asked whether the men had experienced any of the typical symptoms of pregnancy—nausea, weight gain, fatigue, increased appetite, and emotional changes. The couples who were tested were exposed to their newborns, or to blankets that had been in the nursery, and to a film about breast-feeding to see whether the infant cues would cause any short-term change in hormone levels.

The tests revealed significant changes in each of the three hormones Storey and Wynne-Edwards measured—testosterone, cortisol, and prolactin. And the pattern in men was similar to what happens in pregnant women. Men's testosterone levels fell 33 percent when they had their first contact with their babies, compared to measurements taken near the end of their wives' pregnancies.

What could explain this change in testosterone? Many scientists believe that a rise in testosterone is associated with competitive behavior in animals and in men. The drop that occurs with the birth of a baby might be nature's way of encouraging men to drop their fists, at least temporarily, and nuzzle their babies. From an evolutionary perspective, this is smart. Competitiveness is incompatible with nurturing. And men who are more bonded to their babies are more likely to stick around and support them.

Indeed, in September 2013, James K. Rilling and his colleagues at Emory University reported in the *Proceedings of the National Academy of Sciences* that testosterone levels in the blood were inversely correlated with paternal caregiving—that is, testosterone was highest in fathers who devoted less effort to child care, and lowest in those who invested more effort in child care. They also found that the fathers who devoted more resources to their children had smaller testicles. The results provide evidence for the supposition that there is a trade-off between the effort devoted to mating and to parenting. Some males choose to devote more effort to mating and less to child care; others choose the opposite course.

This relationship is seen in animals. Male chimps, who are sexually promiscuous, have testes twice as big as those of humans on average, and they generally don't provide much paternal care. Gorilla males have small testes and guard their young. Human males vary from one individual to another in which approach they are more likely to follow. Rilling's aim with this study was to try to explain why some men are better fathers than others. And while the study doesn't prove that large testicles and elevated testosterone levels can predict what kind of father a man is going to be, it is an important step toward a better understanding of why men vary so widely in the effort they devote to caring for their children.

Storey and her team, in their research on hormonal changes, found other changes in men during their partners' pregnancies—notably, a rise in prolactin near the end of pregnancy. Levels of prolactin were higher in men who showed greater responsiveness to their babies' cries and in men who showed more pregnancy-related symptoms. And there was a clear link between women's hormone levels and those of their partners. Women's hormones rose and fell in connection with the physiological process occurring during pregnancy. Men's hormones rose and fell in accordance with the hormonal changes in their partners.

Women's hormonal changes during pregnancy varied as the time of birth approached. Their hormone levels are associated with the changes going on in their bodies during pregnancy, of course. But fathers' hormonal changes did not correlate with the number of days until birth—they correlated with the hormonal changes in their female partners. This all pointed to the conclusion that the closer and more intimate partners are during pregnancy, the more the man's hormonal shifts parallel those of his partner—and the better a father he becomes.

While this doesn't *prove* a connection between maternal and paternal hormones, it strongly suggests that there is a link, and that these hormonal changes are important for the development of nurturing fathers. Indeed, further research by Storey and Wynne-Edwards has shown that expectant and new fathers who hold their baby—or even a doll wrapped in a blanket that smells of their baby—experience a rise in prolactin and cortisol and a drop in testosterone. The hormones seem to be powerful drivers of men's behavior during pregnancy. It's astonishing that, as far as we can tell, men are mostly unaware of these changes in behavior.

More than hormones are at work, however, in shaping men's relationships with their infants. A father's physical and mental status can also affect an infant's health. In 2010, Prakesh S. Shah of the University of Toronto noted that scant research had been done on whether there was any link between fathers and either preterm infants or those born full-term with low birth weight. (Both outcomes increase the risk of illness or death in the first days and weeks of life.) Most research had been done on mothers, as you might expect, where the possibility of a link between the mother's adverse health or behavior and her infant's outcome might be easier to understand. Mothers' risk factors for adverse outcomes have been studied extensively, for the obvious reason that mothers contribute far more to their children during the nine months of gestation than fathers do. That's a fact of biology. But that doesn't mean fathers should be overlooked.

To remedy the lack of information on fathers, Shah and his colleagues collected thirty-six studies and analyzed them to see what links they might reveal between fathers and birth outcomes. They concluded that these adverse outcomes in babies were more likely to occur as fathers grew older and if the fathers had been born with low birth weight themselves.

The Toronto study was accompanied by a commentary in the same issue of the *American Journal of Obstetrics and Gynecology*, in which another group of researchers criticized the team for not going further. The critics said the scientists had failed to consider a long list of paternal factors that could influence birth outcomes. These include how fathers feel about the pregnancy, their behavior during the pregnancy, and their relationships with the mothers. All of these circumstances can increase mothers' stress during their pregnancies and affect how well they take care of themselves. When fathers don't want to have the baby, mothers are less likely to get prenatal care. Cigarette smoking by fathers can influence a mother's decisions regarding smoking and increase the likelihood of low birth weight.

The commentary marked a rare instance of researchers being publicly criticized for failing to give fathers greater consideration in research. It ended with a recommendation that doctors and scientists devote more attention to fathers when assessing pregnancy risks. It's a good sign: attitudes are changing.

An example of the kind of research the critics were advocating has come out of a group at the University of South Florida led by Amina Alio, a professor of community and public health. She and her colleagues found that fathers who were involved with their partners during pregnancy reduced the risk that the children would die in the first year of life. Infants whose fathers were absent—and had no involvement in the pregnancy—were more likely to be born with lower birth weight and to be born prematurely. The death rate of infants whose fathers were not around was nearly four times that of infants whose fathers *were* involved. And many maternal complications that could affect the infants—such as anemia, high blood pressure, and more serious ailments—were more prevalent among women whose children's fathers were absent.

Yet another study out of New Zealand in 2011 looked at how fathers could affect the birth weight of their children. The group recruited 2,002 couples while the women were pregnant and followed them until birth. Was there a connection, they wondered, between obesity or blood pressure in fathers and the size of their children? Nothing appeared to link blood pressure to birth weight, but something quite startling appeared when they looked at fathers' weight: obesity in fathers, and what's called central obesity, or abdominal fat, were each associated with a 60 percent increase in the risk of having a child with a low birth weight. It didn't matter whether the mother was obese.

This was a revelation. Once fathers have fertilized an egg, they have no physiological connection with their developing fetuses. But somehow they *are* affecting the children's physiology. How does this happen? One guess is that mothers and fathers tend to eat similar diets, and so a father's overeating could influence his partner. Another is that somehow the father's genes are influencing the baby's growth in utero—exactly how that might happen is not known. These discoveries posed yet another challenge to the exclusive research focus on mothers. No one had seen the importance of fathers during pregnancy because investigators had never looked for it.

The new understanding of the biology of fatherhood posed a serious challenge to the mainstream psychological beliefs of the twentieth century. Those beliefs were shaped largely by John Bowlby, who developed one of the most influential and widely accepted psychological descriptions of human development: attachment theory. This grand idea said that an infant's attachment with one caregiver—the mother in almost all cases—was essential for normal psychological growth.

Bowlby began his work in the 1940s. At the time, one of the leading figures in the psychology of parenting was John Watson, who accused parents of being "mawkish" and "sentimental" in their treatment of their children and counseled stern parenting. It's a bad idea to pick up a crying baby, he warned, because that encourages the child to cry more. It was far better to let the baby cry it out. Bowlby's attachment theory drove Watson to the sidelines. Unlike Watson, who thought crying should be discouraged, Bowlby thought it was natural, a kind of protective alarm engineered by natural selection. Babies cry when they need help, food, or protection.

Despite his influence, Bowlby never achieved the popular recognition of his more famous predecessor, Sigmund Freud. Freud was not a scientist, although that's the way he thought of himself. He was a brilliant writer and theorist, but his observations were limited to a very small group of people, almost all of whom came to his attention because they were suffering from a psychiatric disorder. But the timing had been right for Freud's ascendance. Darwin had sought to explain much of biology with simple biological principles, and Freud was trying to do the same thing with human behavior. By the 1950s, nearly every prestigious department of psychiatry in the country was led by a Freudian analyst. They wrote the textbooks, ran the journals, and called the shots.

That's roughly when Bowlby came along to challenge Freud's supremacy. Unlike Freud, Bowlby was a scientist who engaged in conventional research. One of his first projects was a study intended to find out why some children formed secure attachments to their mothers while others didn't. He collaborated with ethologists who were studying parental attachment in animals, to see whether that could shed any light on human attachment. He drew on evolutionary biology, seeking to learn how attachment might affect the likelihood of survival for an animal or a child. And he observed that children who had formed close attachments to their mothers before the age of two were more confident about exploring the world around them, while those who had not were more passive and more likely to cling to their mothers. Children who did not form such secure relationships were likely to suffer from separation anxiety for years to come.

Attachment theory remains one of the foundations of developmental psychology. It made Bowlby the most-cited psychologist in academic journals in the twentieth century, outranking even Freud. It revolutionized the understanding not only of attachment, but also of separation and bereavement. And it focused exclusively on mothers. The role of the father, Bowlby believed, was to provide support for the mother. In the drama of childhood, he was merely a supporting actor. (Shakespeare thought so, too. In his monologue on the seven ages of man beginning with "All the world's a stage," he describes men as infants, children, lovers, soldiers, and more—but never as parents.)

Despite the overwhelming acceptance of attachment theory, it was based primarily on Bowlby's clinical observations of children and parents, not on experiment. It was more scientific than Freud's work, but it hadn't been subject to rigorous evaluation. That job would fall to Mary Ainsworth, a disciple of Bowlby's who worked with him for several years in the early 1950s. Early in her career, she moved to Uganda with her husband, who had been hired by the East African Institute of Social Research in Kampala. When she arrived, she scraped together enough money to do a nine-month study of Ugandan mothers and infants. She concluded that sensitive, responsive mothers, and those who particularly enjoyed breast-feeding, were more likely than other mothers to foster secure attachment in their infants.

Two years later, Ainsworth moved to Baltimore, where she began teaching at Johns Hopkins University and continued her research. She took on a British student named Michael Lamb, who came to the United States because he wanted to study with her. Lamb, now a professor in the Department of Psychology at the University of Cambridge and one of the leading figures in father research, was excited by Ainsworth's work, but puzzled that fathers were being so completely ignored. "These kids they were studying were growing up in two-parent families. They had fathers as well as mothers, but all the focus was on the relationships with the mothers," he told me. "It struck me as odd that there seemed to be this incredibly matricentric assumption in the field. That's what got me started asking about those other relationships."

His initial interest in fathers came not only from his scientific work, but also from his relationship with his own father, who was a hugely important figure in his life. Lamb grew up in Zambia, where his father worked for the British colonial government but came home every day for lunch and spent as much time as he could with his children. The studies that Lamb did under Ainsworth's tutelage were among the first to challenge assumptions about the supporting role of fathers. When he first told Ainsworth he wanted to look at fathers, she tried to discourage him. But he persisted, and did a study which showed that babies and fathers become attached in the same way—and at the same time developmentally—that mothers and babies do.

It was a significant finding, not only for psychologists, but for fathers themselves. "Fathers can hardly be expected to maintain a belief in their importance when they are continually being told of their irrelevance, other than as economic supporters of the family unit," Lamb wrote.

Lamb was one of the first to push back against the conventional wisdom, but far from the last. The study of depression in children is yet another area in which fathers were long overlooked. Psychologists understood that depression in pregnant women can adversely affect their children, but for a long time, nobody seriously entertained the idea that depression in fathers during pregnancy could do the same. But that is changing. Depression in fathers increases the risk of depression in children, just as mothers' depression does—even though fathers have no direct connection with their fetuses during their partners' pregnancies.

Some of the best evidence for the adverse consequences of depression in fathers comes from work done in early 2013 by a research team in Norway led by Anne Lise Kvalevaag. She sifted through data on 31,663 children and their families to collect information on fathers' mental health during pregnancy. Studies such as these look for associations; they don't say anything about why such associations might exist. The researchers suggested three possibilities: The fathers could be passing on to their children genes that are associated with psychological problems. The fathers' depression could be having an influence on their partners, which could in turn have an effect on the children. Or the children's problems might be a result of paternal depression during their infancy and early childhood: fathers who are depressed before birth are more likely than others to be depressed afterward, too. Whatever the explanation, all this work suggested that fathers' mental health can indeed have important consequences for their children.

And the outcome can be even worse for the unfortunate children who have two depressed parents. Researchers at Cincinnati Children's Hospital Medical Center showed that if both parents are depressed, children have eight times the risk of behavioral or emotional problems of children whose parents are not depressed. Many studies have shown that poor mental health in mothers has negative impacts on children's behavior and emotional health, but few studies have looked at both parents.

There is some good news here. A healthy father can ease the impact of a mother's depression on their children. He can serve as a buffer, engaging the children when mother isn't available because of her illness. But that's not easy to do. Mothers do a lot for their children, and if they're compromised by illness, they aren't easy to replace. Depression often carries with it a good deal of guilt, and mothers or fathers who are depressed around the time of their children's birth may carry the additional burden of knowing that they cannot fully engage with their children and might be putting them at risk of emotional problems of their own later on.

The list of unfortunate consequences of fathers' depression continues to grow. A mother's depression is known to be related to excessive crying, or colic, in infants, but the role of depression in fathers was unknown. When Mijke P. van den Berg of Erasmus Medical Center in the Netherlands took a look, he found that paternal depression was indeed a risk factor for excessive crying in infants. The explanation is unclear. It could be something in the father's genetic makeup that he is passing on, his altered interaction with the infant, or marital or family stress related to the depression. Whatever the case, the study emphasizes the importance of considering fathers when studying infant behavior, including excessive crying. Yet another study found that depressed fathers were more likely to spank their children and less likely to read to them than fathers without depression.

·

Conflict between mothers and fathers can also interfere with infants' well-being. In the late 1990s, James P. McHale, a family therapist now at the University of South Florida St. Petersburg, conducted a research project at Clark University in Massachusetts sponsored by the National Institutes of Health called Families Through Time, in which he explored how mothers' and fathers' coparenting relationships affected their children. It was the first study to look at the development of the coparenting alliance in intact (not divorced) families. One of the things McHale and his colleagues recognized from the outset was that they should investigate parents' relationships during the mothers' pregnancy. Research had suggested that the personalities of the parents, their thoughts about intimate relationships, and the quality of the marriage were all important. But McHale thought there was another ingredient that researchers had overlooked. "The missing element was parents' perspectives on what family life ought to be like and what they hoped to create individually and together with their partner in the new family."

McHale, who says his work was inspired by the Cowans, recognized that a key ingredient to family health that had been missing from prior research was an understanding of the coparenting alliance adults formed with respect to their children. The idea behind his study—and one that was borne out by his research—was that when parents have a strong alliance, children show fewer signs of stress, marital relationships are stronger, and children have better relationships with their peers. Other researchers had studied coparenting in divorced families, in which parents try to work out arrangements that reduce conflict, but nobody had looked closely at families in which the parents are still

together. In many families, "both parents have good relationships with the kids, but still the kid is in turmoil, and it's
often because of the coparenting relationship . . . Two parents can hate each other and try to win the child's affection
and loyalty." This kind of chronic child-related conflict often
leads to a poor outcome for the child, as one might expect.
Many divorced families fit this pattern, but so do one in five
intact families, according to McHale.

One of the first things he found was that the coparenting
beliefs of parents-to-be were shaped by their experiences
with their own parents and families growing up. "My family
always had family days on Sunday," said one parent, Candice.
"I want us to be doing the same things, too, as a family."
Her husband, Ron, agreed with her about Sunday dinners,
but not about child care. "She'll handle most of the child-
care responsibilities," he said. "She's going to be a stay-at-
home mom, and I'm hoping she'll change all the diapers."

Candice said, "I'll be the primary caregiver during the
day, but when he gets home, he'll take over . . . I think he'll
be a very involved dad because his father wasn't." Ron said
his parents "argued about us kids a lot. I don't want us to
re-create the kinds of arguments that I always used to experience between my parents." Clearly, unless they begin to
talk about their coparenting, Ron and Candice are set up
for a serious confrontation about Ron's obligations as a father. McHale called the disagreements "potential flash-
points."

McHale and his team assessed depression and marital
satisfaction in the expectant parents at the beginning of the
third trimester before their child's birth. They were surprised to discover far more strain than they had anticipated.
Forty percent of the mothers and 22 percent of the fathers

scored high on a test designed to assess depression. After examining the survey results, the researchers hypothesized that the tests may have actually reflected not depression as much as general anxiety about impending parenthood. "At a minimum, a great many parents in our sample were experiencing jitters," McHale wrote. "Quite often these were significant levels of jitters, and many experienced much more than that." Marital satisfaction was less of an issue, with only a handful reporting problems. But when the researchers added up all the numbers, they found that at least one parent in half of the families reported concerns with symptoms of depression or strains in their marriage.

As the Cowans, McHale, and others talked with expectant fathers, one thing that emerged was the determination of the fathers to "be there" both physically and emotionally for their children, as many felt their traditional fathers had not been for them. "This is what men look forward to about having a baby," wrote the Cowans, "and it is what they worry about while they are waiting."

These men have the right idea. But they needn't wait until their children are born to get involved. A father who helps his pregnant partner buy supplies, takes her to doctors' visits, and sees the fetus on an ultrasound or hears its heartbeat is more likely to be involved with his partner and baby after the birth than one who doesn't have that kind of involvement. This is true even of fathers who don't live with their partners. Fathers who are involved during pregnancy are also more likely to play with and read to the baby, and generally to help take care of the baby. They are more likely to find employment if they are out of work. And if they live

elsewhere, they are more likely to move in with their partners. These ripple effects are good for the parents *and* for
the children.

Wanting to be involved, however, doesn't always trans-
late into *being* involved. When expectant fathers are asked
how they expect to divide chores and child care once their
baby is born, most say they expect mothers to do more, but
think they will make a substantial contribution. Six months
after their children are born, most say mothers are doing
more than expected and they are doing less. Part of the reason could be that fathers are too quick to accept that they
are less important to their children than mothers are. It could
also be that, as with Ron and Candice, they and their partners
disagree about what kind of relationship the father should
have with his children. This raises an important question: Is
it possible to intervene with families to get fathers more involved? Can the beliefs of expectant parents be changed so
that they put more value on the relationships of fathers with
their kids? What effect will that have on the children?

The Cowans partnered with another husband-wife research team, the Yale child psychiatrist Kyle D. Pruett and
Marsha Kline Pruett, a clinical psychologist at Smith College
in Massachusetts, to find out. They knew that fathers are often excluded from efforts by family service agencies to promote healthy pregnancies, and they wanted to see whether
changing that approach could elicit more downstream participation in family life by the fathers. So they devised a
program of sixteen weekly sessions for expectant couples
to help them work on their relationships both as partners
and as parents-to-be. They offered the program to 289 couples from low- and middle-income Mexican-American and
European-American families in five California counties.

Previous research had identified some of the factors
that helped fathers become more involved with their families and children. Among them were many we've already
discussed: the quality of the relationship between the parents, their mental health and stress levels, and the patterns
they had witnessed in their own parents and grandparents.
Various groups, including government agencies and religious organizations, had devised fatherhood workshops of
some sort. Most were led by male speakers and counselors.
The problem with these programs, according to the Cowans and the Pruetts, was "that the single most powerful predictor of fathers' engagement with their children is the
quality of the men's relationship with the child's mother,
regardless of whether the couple is married, divorced, separated, or never married."

The researchers tried offering their program to fathers
only, and also to mothers and fathers together, to see which
might work better. The program, based on an earlier inter-
vention developed by the Cowans, included exercises, discussions, and short presentations led by male and female pairs
of mental-health professionals. The discussions covered
parenting, the couples' relationships, and stresses and support
outside the family.

The program was most successful when it was given to
mothers and fathers together. Their children were "much
less likely to show signs of depression, anxiety, and hyperactivity," the researchers said. The program also decreased
parenting stress and improved the parents' relationships.
Some of the couples were so enthusiastic about the program
that they continued meeting on their own after the project
was completed.

Pregnancy is a key time for an expectant father to become involved with his partner and with the creature they can see on ultrasound and his partner can feel kicking and moving inside her. This might not ease the financial worries and other fears that can plague men during pregnancy, but it could put them on a path to becoming the fathers they want to be.

When we rid ourselves of the things we *think* we know about fathers, and replace them with what we're now learning, we can do more to encourage fathers to become involved with their children. How many men understand that they are experiencing hormonal changes during their wives' pregnancies? How many understand that being involved with the pregnancy is an important step on the way to being more involved with the child? The idea of the egalitarian family, which many couples say they accept, still outruns the reality. The more we learn about fathers, the more we can bring the idea and the reality together.

FOUR

Fathers in the Lab: Of Mice and Men

I'm standing in a laboratory at Randolph-Macon College in Ashland, Virginia, watching a caged mouse desperately trying to escape. Catherine Franssen, a postdoctoral researcher, has just slipped on a pair of rubber gloves, picked up a few mice, and dropped them into shoebox-size clear plastic cages lined with wood shavings. She's putting the mouse fathers, with their pups, into unfamiliar cages—an exercise the mice don't like. The idea is to see how the fathers will react to the stress in the presence of their pups.

Some of the mice are huddling nervously but one of them is jumping frantically up and down, trying to launch himself over the side to what he thinks will be freedom. What's remarkable about this mouse is that he doesn't show any interest in including his pups in his escape plans. As he jumps up and down, he occasionally lands on top of them. They can't walk yet, so they can't get out of the way. This doesn't concern their father in the least. He continues leaping for the top of the cage.

On the reasonable assumption that few human fathers would be interested in donating their brains to science during their partners' pregnancy or when their children are

born, researchers have resorted to animals to find out what
makes fathers behave the way they do. Studying mice might
seem like a stretch. Humans and rodents don't have a great
deal of mutual affection. When we meet, we're more likely
to turn and run in opposite directions. But think about this
the next time you set a mousetrap: humans and mice share
90 percent of their genes. Mice are not as close to us, genetically, as chimpanzees, but they're not far behind.

Franssen works with Kelly G. Lambert, a neuroscientist
and the head of the psychology department at Randolph-
Macon. I sat down with Lambert on a warm spring day, just
after classes had ended, and asked her how reliable a proxy
the mouse brain was for a human's gray matter. She promptly
opened a refrigerator in her lab, grabbed a pair of tweezers,
pulled a mouse brain out of a little plastic vial, and set it
down gently on a paper towel. It was pale yellow, furrowed,
and about the size of a marble. And it was shaped just like a
miniature human brain.

Lambert said that if she were to carefully dissect the
brain and spread it out on the table, she would find all the
structures found in the human brain. There *are* differences.
Most of them can be found in the cortex, the site of many
higher brain functions. "There is a huge difference between
the rat and the human, and even chimps and humans, in the
complexity of the cortex," Lambert notes. And of course
the mouse brain is much smaller. If she were to flatten and
spread out the cortex of the mouse brain, it would be smaller
than a postage stamp. If she did the same thing with a human
cortex, it would cover most of a coffee table.

Nevertheless, Lambert's work is based on the proposition that mice can teach us an enormous amount about
human behavior. "I'm looking at stress and resilience and

parental behavior, coping, how the brain responds to enriched environments. They've got so much genetic similarity. And I can control for diet and age, control we are never going to have with humans. They can give us clues we just can't pick up with humans."

Lambert has a lot riding on the answer. She's spent twenty-five years designing experiments to let "rodents speak their mind," as she puts it. She refers to her lab animals as her "rodent colleagues," and observes that she is among the minority of humans who have had "valuable professional relationships with rodents." When she's thinking about human behavior, she often asks herself: "What Would Rodents Do?"

Their virtue is that they don't have a cover story. "When I assess a rodent, I get the real deal—pure, unadulterated, raw behavior. When I'm working with rats, I ask a question and get the answer," Lambert says. Humans, she says, are quite different. They have a remarkable ability to fabricate stories to justify their behavior. In one study, for example, women said their children were among the things in their lives that made them happiest. But the same women said that child care was one of their least favorite activities. Apparently, not everything about babies is so enchanting after all. Lambert says she doesn't get that kind of double talk from her rodents. The father I saw stomping on his pups, for instance, wasn't the least bit self-conscious about his lack of interest in his kids.

Rodents are also remarkably sophisticated, as Lambert likes to point out. Until a few years ago, researchers believed that only humans and other primates—gorillas and chimps, for example—were capable of metacognition, which means, roughly, that they know what they know and what they don't. But in 2007, Jonathon Crystal and colleagues at the University of Georgia tested rats' ability to discriminate between long and short sounds. Rats that could tell the difference got a reward. Those that failed the test got nothing.

Then the researchers gave the rats a third option: if, based on their training, they weren't sure whether a sound was long or short, they could opt not to take the test—which would get them a small reward. Amazingly, researchers found that some rats declined to take the test, opting for the smaller reward rather than gambling on all or nothing. And when the test was made more difficult, more rats opted out. The rats were able to tell whether they would likely pass the test—they understood what they were capable of. This ranks them ahead of middle-aged fathers who think they might run a 10K, only to reconsider after huffing and puffing their way to the end of the block.

Lambert began her studies of rat parents with an effort to understand how females make the switch from ensuring their own survival to ensuring that of their offspring. She and Craig Howard Kinsley, a colleague at the University of Richmond in Virginia, reasoned that a variety of circuits must start to fire in a rat's brain when she becomes a mother. A mother must take risks to protect her young, sometimes leaving the pups alone to find food, exposing them to predators. In the effort to find food, she might be exposing herself to predators, too. Lambert and Kinsley guessed that the rat's foraging skills would improve when she becomes a mother, because she would need to squelch any fear and anxiety, get out there and grab some food for the kids, and hightail it back to the nest before a hawk could sink its deadly talons into one of her pups or a snake swallow one whole.

The operation had to be as efficient as possible to reduce the risks for her young.

Lambert and Kinsley conducted a series of experiments that proved their hunch was correct. When female rats became mothers, they developed enhanced spatial learning and memory. As she and Kinsley wrote, young rats that had been mothers once or twice "were much better than age-matched virgin rats at remembering the location of a food reward in two different kinds of mazes." Lambert and Kinsley didn't stop there. Next, they put females who had never been pregnant together with pups, turning the females into rat foster mothers. The foster mothers showed the same improvement in the maze as the biological mothers! Simply being in the *presence* of offspring—their own or somebody else's—turned female rats into better foragers.

Some of Kinsley's students also found that motherhood turned rats into better hunters. The students put hungry females into a five-foot-square enclosure in which a cricket—a treat for rats—had been hidden in the wood chips. Females that had never been pregnant took an average of 270 seconds to find and eat the cricket; lactating females did it in just over 50 seconds. The researchers also found that the mothers were less likely to freeze up or otherwise demonstrate fear while exploring the unfamiliar enclosure during the experiment. And they found reduced activity in portions of the hippocampus and amygdala, parts of the brain the regulate stress and emotion.

Lambert and her team also found some of the first evidence that having children could make mothers better multitaskers, a change that many human mothers would insist is true whatever the evidence might show. (And the evidence increasingly suggests that it *is* true.) The researchers set up a race to find a reward—a Froot Loop, as it happens—that involved "simultaneously monitoring sights, sounds, odors, and other animals." The mothers who had been pregnant at least twice did far better than mothers who'd been pregnant once, and all of them did better than the hapless virgins. The more time the mothers spent with pups, the more skilled they became.

I did not go to see Lambert only to talk about mothers. When her work on females was published, I called to ask whether she planned to do similar research on male rodents. "We're just beginning," she told me. I waited until she had some results before driving down from New York to see her. For the research on fathers, rats wouldn't work. Rat fathers don't hang around. She calls them "drive-through dads." So she switched to the California mouse, a species with devoted fathers, and the closely related deer mouse, for whom fatherhood is a far more casual affair. And then she began to do some of the same kinds of experiments she'd done with her rat mothers.

Male California mice, a species known scientifically as *Peromyscus californicus*, groom, retrieve, and huddle with their offspring—all the things that a good mouse father should do. And their care shapes the behavior of their pups. James P. Curley of Columbia University notes that paternal grooming is essential for young mice to be able to recognize new objects. Pups that are not properly groomed have difficulty with that task, and they show detrimental changes in stress hormones as well. Fathers' behavior also appears to be related to the kind of paternal care their offspring will later provide when they become fathers themselves. Good fatherhood, of the type practiced by the California mouse, has numerous benefits for pups.

The situation is different, however, in one of the California mouse's closest relatives—the common deer mouse, or *Peromyscus maniculatus*. The deer mouse is brown with a white underbelly, and not much longer than your index finger. And he is not a model father. Quite the opposite. This was the mouse that I watched trying to leap his way out of his cage while only occasionally paying his floppy pink-and-gray pups a brief bit of attention—stretching his head out to give them a sniff before scrambling away to resume his escape attempts. The deer mouse's pathetic escape attempts and his lack of concern for his flesh and blood are typical of the behavior of mammal fathers, only a few of which have any interest in their offspring. The odd behavior of the deer mouse was a good reminder of how unusual human fathers are.

In a nearby cage, a California mouse father was demonstrating why Lambert had chosen this species to study. He is far from typical of mice and other mammals, and she wanted to find out what it was about him, his brain, and his hormones that made him so different. While we watched, he nervously explored his new environment, whiskers vigorously twitching, but he never left the pups alone for more than a few seconds. He inspected them, licked them, hovered over them, crouched near them while raising his head to look for threats, and regularly hunched his back and leaned over them again, like a bird perched on its eggs.

If I hadn't known he was the father, I would have thought I was watching a mother protect her young long after the father has fled, as most mammal fathers do. Franssen confirmed my impression. She told me that his behavior was often indistinguishable from that of a California mouse mother. With the mother away in a different cage, the pups even nipped at their father's underside, looking for a nipple to latch on to. It was fruitless. Male California mice have vestigial mammary glands, but they lack even the nonfunctional nipples that human fathers have. Lactation (and pregnancy) remain out of reach for these devoted fathers, but in other respects, the fathers among California mice do everything for their children that mothers do.

The differences in the paternal behavior of these two closely related species were discovered in the late 1980s and early 1990s by a psychologist named David Gubernick, first at Indiana University and then at the University of Wisconsin. Gubernick came to his research with an unusual background. He did his graduate work in psychology, but did postdoctoral study in zoology, which equipped him to look at two things in mouse family life: the immediate factors that could affect behavior (that's psychology) and the evolutionary roots of that behavior (the perspective of zoologists).

To learn about the California mouse at a study site near Monterey, California, he needed to set scores of traps in the field, capture the mice, tag them, and release them. "You set up a grid, where you have two live traps, metal rectangular shapes that have a folding door in front. And when the animal walks in to get food in the back, the door slams shut. You have lines of traps that maybe are ten yards apart or so." Gubernick and his colleagues then crawled around on the ground, sometimes in the mud, opening these traps, making measurements, and releasing the mice.

In the winter, Gubernick would place a small wad of

cotton bedding in the traps to help keep the animals warm. The scientists weren't so lucky. "It can be miserable if it's raining and cold," he says. "You have a headlamp on, and a handheld ultraviolet light, and you're marking these animals with little numbered ear tags to identify each individual." And opening the trap can be a surprise. "Sometimes you get other mice in there, sometimes insects, and other animals who might try to put their nose in the trap and close it." All the fieldwork is done at night, in the dark, because that's when the animals are active.

Gubernick dusted females with different colors of pigmented powder, using pigments visible only in ultraviolet light. Matching the colors that rubbed off on the males with the females after they had mated in the wild showed who they nested with; later genetic testing demonstrated for the first time that they were strictly monogamous—the male paired with the female was the father of all her offspring. "It may be the only truly monogamous thing in California," Gubernick cracked.

The fieldwork built on his earlier laboratory findings, in which he had bred the mice and removed the fathers from their mates and offspring. The idea was to see whether their absence would have adverse consequences for the pups. The results were a little more complicated—and more interesting—than you might think.

Gubernick set up three sets of conditions: a warm room with food and water; a warm room where parents were required to work for food (that is, they had to run on a wheel before food would be dispensed); and a cold room where they were likewise required to work for food—to mimic winter conditions. With food and a warm room, removing the father had no effect. Where fathers had to work for food or perform in a cold room, they clearly enhanced the pups' survival. These circumstances, in which fathers were shown to make a difference, more closely resembled natural conditions.

Next, the researchers did the experiment in the field, with similar results. They removed the males from half of a selected group of nests, and left the males in the other half. Fewer young emerged from the nests in father-absent families than in father-present families—indicating that without a father's care, more were dying. The reason for the increased survival in father-present nests was the direct parental care provided by the fathers. Male parental care presumably evolved because it was critical for survival of the offspring. Gubernick says his study was "the first demonstration in the wild that males were indeed necessary for offspring survival." Additional data showed that the primary importance of fathers was not for protection but to provide direct care of their young.

Gubernick has also shown that males engage in as much parental activity as females, licking pups, carrying them, and huddling over them. Those activities keep the young warm—a critical factor in survival because the pups can't regulate their own body temperatures until they are about two weeks old. And he also found that prolactin—the hormone associated with nursing—was elevated in fathers after the birth of their offspring. We've already seen that it rises in birds, other rodents, and humans. The prolactin levels of the male California mice were the same as those of mothers, suggesting that prolactin levels correlate with the fathers' parental behavior.

•

The differences in the paternal behavior of California mice and deer mice were easy to see in Lambert's laboratory. But identifying the differences in their brains that gave rise to their behavior would require months of experimentation. Lambert and her students set up their experiments so the mouse fathers—the good and the bad—were separated from other mice, including their pups, for twenty-four hours, and then exposed to their own pups, to somebody else's pups— these were so-called foster dads—or to brothers they'd been raised with. This last group would serve as the control, because those males wouldn't be exposed to any young mice at all.

The idea to separate the fathers and pups before the experiment came from Lambert's reflections on her own parenting. "The more I thought about it, I realized that my circuits are most activated when I've been separated from my kids—and reunited. So we thought, we're going to separate everybody for twenty-four hours from their brothers or their families. And then we'll put them into the cage with their own pups or just their brothers, so we could see if the brain changes occur when they came across any familiar animal or just the pups."

Once the team had done these experiments, they sacrificed the fathers and dissected their brains, making extremely thin slices and examining them to see which neurons were active. "It's kind of like a PET scan," Lambert explained. They also determined whether the fathers' brains were restructuring or growing new neurons as the mice became fathers, or foster fathers in the case of those exposed to others' pups.

They ran similar experiments with mothers, so had some sense of what they might see with fathers. "We had found that the moms had some plasticity—some changes were happening in their brains," Lambert told me. "Our moms were better foragers, and bolder. And there were increased connections in neurons in the hippocampus. That's involved in learning and memory, including spatial learning." It's what mothers need to become the efficient foragers that they are, more skillful than their virgin counterparts.

The research with the fathers showed much the same thing. Not only were the California mouse fathers behaving like the mothers, they were also experiencing the same kinds of changes in the brain. The control mice who weren't fathers and hadn't been exposed to pups didn't show the same brain changes. The good dads had reduced neural activity in parts of the brain associated with stress, and increased activity in a couple of brain hormones—vasopressin and oxytocin. Interestingly, the researchers found that the foster dads showed some—but not all—of the brain changes seen in the biological fathers. Just being around pups, in other words, was enough to make a male's brain partially resemble the brains of the good biological dads. It was similar to what Lambert had seen in her rodent mothers—being around pups produced changes in their behavior.

When they tried the same experiment with deer mice—the bad fathers—they found a much different picture. The dads and the foster dads were not distinguishable—both lacked many of the fathering-related brain changes seen in the California mice. These fathers have the circuitry and the neurochemistry to behave like good fathers. But they don't exploit that circuitry to take care of their pups.

After the demonstration with the deer mouse and the California mouse, Franssen put the animals back in their proper cages. We gathered around a table in the lab, and I asked why there should be such a great difference between two species so closely related.

The hypothesis is that the difference arises from some critical features of the way the two species live. A father will stick around if his presence does something useful for his offspring. "If you can provide evidence that the offspring are healthier or better off when the father is there, then it's adaptive for him to be there," Lambert said. We're all wired to pass on our genes, and males will do what they must to give their progeny the best chance of survival.

The California mice live in a desertlike strip of the state. It gets very hot during the day and very cold at night. The mothers leave their pups to forage at night, when it's cold, so the fathers have to be there to keep the babies warm. It's a reminder that studies of the brain ought to consider the brain in context. "It's the same with humans," Lambert explains. "Is the dad bringing something to the table? It doesn't have to be money; it can be social interactions, intellectual strategies, or enriching life in some way." If so, and it helps the children survive, it makes sense for the family to have evolved in such a way that the father hangs around.

If the father can't do anything to boost his children's prospects, he's not going to stay around. That's why, for example, vulnerable young turtles are left alone for the perilous crawl from nests on the beach into the sea. In this extreme case, neither mothers nor fathers can do anything to protect them. Lumbering awkwardly along the sand in their shells, they can't groom their young or huddle to keep them warm the way the California mouse can. So the best strategy for turtles is to begin preparing immediately to have more offspring, rather than trying and failing to protect those they've already produced.

•

Lambert and Franssen are not the only researchers looking to mice for answers to key questions about human males. Heidi S. Fisher and Hopi E. Hoekstra of Harvard University have been particularly interested in the *promiscuity* of deer mice. A female can mate with one male, and then another, and keep on going at a rate of more than one male per minute. How long the female can continue this sexual marathon isn't clear. That's because Fisher and Hoekstra didn't follow the females. They followed the sperm. They found that the reproductive tracts of female deer mice were filled with sperm from multiple partners, but the sperm from each male could recognize their genetically related "siblings" as they swam upstream. "Brother" sperm from the same male tended to clump together, joining forces to try to penetrate the egg. The sperm best able to cooperate in this way boosted their chances of beating a competing male's sperm to the egg. Fisher and Hoekstra found that deer mouse sperm have sickle-shaped heads topped with hooks that enable them to link up, forming tangled clumps with multiple wriggling tails. Other sperm were doing the same thing—hooking up with *their* kin—to make the competition that much keener.

The clincher came when the researchers looked at another closely related mouse, the oldfield mouse (*Peromyscus polionotus*, if you're keeping score). This mouse is monogamous, and its sperm don't have the ability to recognize and link to one another. But the monogamous mouse father doesn't need that ability—there are no other sperm in the female's reproductive tract, so it's not a battleground for warring sperm from different sexual partners.

One of the most remarkable things Lambert sees in *her* mouse fathers is a conceptual leap from caring only for themselves to caring for someone else. "The mammalian leap to caring for others is something I'm fascinated by. You've extended your concern for survival to another being. Humans are right up there with [other] mammals that have a long childhood. Parenting is a long-term investment for humans. The more help you have, the more insurance you have. If nothing else, one parent could die. You have a backup." And, importantly, each parent treats the children a little differently. "They're complementing each other. This is great. It's complex, and it's interesting."

Many animals have something to teach us about fatherhood—even those that are more distantly related to us than rats and mice, which should feel like cousins by now. Those animal species in which fathers do contribute to rearing the kids have found many different ways to carry out that mission. The one thing that they share, from seahorses to penguins to poison frogs, is that they all perform some essential function that helps their offspring survive. And by studying these essential contributions, we get some perspective on human fathering. Our way of doing things is not the only way.

One of the most famous animal fathers is the emperor penguin, whose epic fathering was featured in the Academy Award–winning documentary, *March of the Penguins*. When these monogamous penguins breed, fathers hold their partners' eggs close to protect them from the unimaginably cold and black Antarctic winter. While fathers are guarding the eggs, the mothers march up to 100 miles to the ocean, where they eat their fill in preparation for feeding the hatchlings that will be waiting for them when they return to their partners. The fathers stand huddled together on sea ice in vast numbers for almost three months, trying to shield one another from knife-sharp winds and barely endurable temperatures. The fathers, lacking a nest to sit on, balance the single egg—each of which weighs up to a pound—on their feet, underneath a flap of feathered skin. There the eggs are kept at a temperature of about 95 degrees Fahrenheit—even when the temperature outside falls to 95 below zero.

One of the themes of *March of the Penguins* was the devotion between the parents. They make a serious contract with each other—the father trades protection of the egg for an abundant supply of baby food from the mother. For this to work, marital fidelity is required on the part of both parents, or the system would never have evolved as it did. But is the emperor penguin really monogamous? The film, ending with the joyful reunions of mother and father, leaves us wondering about what comes next.

The reality is that the reunions aren't quite so joyful. When a mother returns from collecting food in the sea, she sings as she wanders through thousands of males, until she finds her mate. (If the mother is late in returning—most mothers return, incredibly, on the day their eggs hatch—the father regurgitates something called penguin milk, secreted by the lining of his esophagus, into the newborn's beak.) The birds do a little dance, stand immobile for a few minutes, and then circle around each other, while the mother looks at the father's flap of feathers, shielding the egg.

There the inspirational family story ends. According to the writer Jeffrey Moussaieff Masson, "The male allows the egg to fall gently to the ice, whereupon the female takes it and then turns her back to the male, to whom, after a final duet, she becomes completely indifferent." The male "stares at his empty pouch, pecks at it with his beak, lifts up his head, groans, and then pecks the female. She shows no further interest in him and eventually he leaves for the open sea, to break his long fast. The whole affair has lasted about eighty minutes." The following year, they mate again—but almost always with different partners.

This might seem like a poor outcome for a father who has starved himself during the harshest weather to protect his offspring, even if he has succeeded in reproducing. But as Kelly Lambert argues, it's the brain, or the behavior, *in context* that matters. Penguin fathers endure the Antarctic winter because they have no choice; their behavior has evolved to help their offspring survive in a tough neighborhood. That survival is their reward.

The seahorse takes a far more bizarre route to good fatherhood. A favorite in aquariums, and the animal kingdom's poster child for exemplary fatherhood, it is an extreme example of how far fatherhood can go: in seahorses, it is the male that gets pregnant. The female faces him, and they bend their tails back. She then inserts her ovipositor (it looks like a penis) into the male's open pouch and releases a long, sticky string of eggs—hundreds of them. The male seals the pouch shut.

The seahorse was once thought to be the only animal in which the male became pregnant, but more recently scientists have discovered that the same is true of the male pipefish, a seahorse relative. In a particularly nasty example of parental favoritism, the pregnant pipefish father doles out nutrients to the offspring he's carrying based on what he "thinks" of their mother. A father who has mated with a particularly attractive female, whatever that means to a pipefish (apparently, the bigger the better) will devote more resources to his offspring, and more of them will survive, than if he had mated with a female less likely to produce quality stock.

In some species of poison frogs, the females lay eggs and the fathers carry them on their backs to a watery hollow, where they drop them into the water. Some of these pools are smaller than a shot glass. The male monitors the tadpoles that emerge—sometimes helping them break the egg sac. He monitors the food supply and will call the female if the tadpoles need to be fed. The female returns and lays a specialized kind of egg that is eaten by the tadpoles. Males of other frog species pick the eggs up and hold them in their mouths, where the tadpoles develop, finding food in the father's mouth. When they've developed into tiny frogs, they hop out. The male midwife toad carries strings of eggs attached to his legs, and when they hatch, he drops the tadpoles into ponds. Male bullfrogs will chase away snakes ten times their size to protect their young.

No discussion of animal fathers would be complete without a nod to marmosets and tamarins, among the world's smallest—and most captivating—monkeys. They live in the tropics of the Western Hemisphere, they are monogamous, and they almost always have twins—twice a year. At birth, the babies weigh as much as a fifth of their mother's body weight. And she will soon be pregnant with another pair, so after the babies are born, the fathers cart them around. It's hard work, and the dads lose up to a tenth of their body weight doing it.

Charles T. Snowdon of the University of Wisconsin has shown that most cotton-top tamarin fathers start carrying infants the day they are born. Interestingly, the fathers got help from the infants' older brothers, and by the time the infants were four weeks old, their brothers spent more time carrying them than their fathers did. Mothers did little to help, but they were capable of shifting gears when circumstances demanded it. In families in which fathers were absent, mothers took over, with help from older siblings, especially brothers. In a separate study, Snowdon also showed that in a frightening situation, when a lab worker wearing a white coat and an animal mask approached the cage, the infants ran to the adult who had carried and fed them the most—either the father or their oldest brother. And as we've seen with humans, marmoset and tamarin fathers experience couvade—they gain weight during their mates' pregnancies, presumably bulking up to prepare for carrying around those expected kids.

These animal fathers have the good fortune to be present at the births of their offspring, as human fathers often are, too. But allowing men into delivery rooms, which we now take for granted, is a relatively new phenomenon, going back only a generation or so. Many women find it comforting to have their husbands with them during labor and delivery, and men who participate in birth are more likely to participate in the care of their infants. It seems to be a winning proposition all around. It also allows parents to share one of the most intense emotional experiences they will ever have. I can't imagine how I would feel if I'd missed it.

Men who had once been in their own homes for the births of their children were exiled when childbirth moved out of the home and into hospitals, a movement that accelerated in the 1930s. By the 1960s, 99 percent of white children and 85 percent of nonwhite children were born in hospitals. This was supposed to lead to safer childbirth and healthier children. Fathers were left pacing in waiting rooms while their wives and a phalanx of professionals attended the birth and kept the father out.

Followers of *I Love Lucy* reruns will remember the episodes dealing with Lucille Ball's pregnancy in the early 1950s, when pregnancy was rarely shown in television sitcoms. The seven episodes that dealt with Lucy's pregnancy weren't limited to the drama and comedy of the expectant mother. Her husband Ricky's reactions were featured in the episodes, too. Ricky thinks he's suffering labor pains in one episode—perhaps the first televised depiction of couvade—and to make him feel better, Lucy and her neighbors Fred and Ethel throw him a "daddy shower." When it's time to race to the hospital to have the baby, however, Ricky is stopped in the waiting room, where he signs papers, pays the bill, and paces.

By the 1960s, men wanted in. Many hospitals argued that they didn't have room for men in the labor room. "At first," the historian Judith Walzer Leavitt writes, quoting the pioneering birth activist Elly Rakowitz, "no one wanted to take the responsibility of allowing fathers to be present in labor rooms. Doctors would say it was up to the hospitals; hospitals would pass the buck back to the doctors." If men did get permission to be present for labor, it was only "*if* the obstetrical floor isn't busy, and *if* there is no laboring woman in the other bed in the room, and *if* prenatal classes had been attended . . . if, if, if."

Men began to earn their place in the labor room, but they were still excluded from the delivery of their children. I was surprised to find out what some fathers went through to attend the births of their children. One father, a bus driver in Portland, Oregon who refused to remain in the waiting room, went to court in the 1960s to establish his right to be present at his child's birth. When he made his argument in the courtroom, he got a standing ovation. By 1975, men had made some progress, with about three-quarters of hospitals allowing them into the delivery room—except in the South, where barely more than a quarter did so.

Many obstetricians still frowned on the practice, worrying that laymen might challenge their medical decisions without understanding the reasons for them. One said a man wouldn't let him use forceps and threatened to kill him if his wife and the baby were not okay. Another physician berated a nurse, telling her that "one of your G.D. [goddamn] fathers was at a delivery this morning and he wouldn't let me give Pitocin." The physician called the police and had the man removed. Despite doctors' discomfort, by the end of the 1970s most restrictions had been relaxed, and organizations of obstetricians, nurses, nurse-midwives, and hospitals were promoting the practice of letting men in.

Not all fathers were in favor of this development. Some said they were shocked at the appearance of their newborns, pickled in their juices and specked with blood. One said his baby looked "like a newborn rat." Very quickly, however, researchers noticed and began to chart a fascinating and unexpected side effect of fathers' presence in the delivery room: women reported that they felt less pain, and they needed less pain medication. Women were less likely to cry—and fathers were *more* likely to cry.

One nurse said she thought that was because fathers were taking over the job of worrying about whether the baby has the right number of fingers and toes, an examination

I'm proud to say I performed on each of my children within seconds of their birth. I let the doctors worry about Apgar scores; I had my own checklist. Beyond that, it's now clear that fathers' presence matters. Those who are present for their children's birth are more attached to their children, and they later become more involved in taking care of their infants, a development that seems likely to benefit not only the father but also the mother and, most important, the child. Letting fathers into the delivery room pays off in ways no one anticipated.

The last remaining roadblock for fathers around the end of the 1970s was getting permission to be present in the operating room for a cesarean section. Some fathers, newly admitted to delivery rooms in that decade, found themselves spending hours in the labor room with their wives, only to be suddenly excluded from the birth when the obstetrician had to perform a C-section. Women argued for men to be allowed into the operating room. As late as 1980, most hospitals were still barring fathers from the OR.

My first child was born in 1981. When the obstetrician called for an emergency C-section, a nurse helped me awkwardly step into a surgical gown and slip on a mask. I was walked carefully to a stool behind a partial curtain, so I couldn't see the actual birth. When the time came, I cheated. I stood up and peeked over the curtain to watch the obstetrician pull our son out through the incision, crying, wrinkled, and waxy. I had no idea until I began the research for this book that if he'd been born only two or three years earlier, I probably would have missed that. I've now been in the operating room for five C-sections. I've looked over the curtain every time, and if it weren't for the lack of a medical license, I might be ready to try doing one myself.

•

I've seen so many births because I had three children, now grown, with my first wife, and two with my second. Those of us who have been married more than once might pose a challenge to an important observation by anthropologists: Humans are predominantly monogamous. But our version of monogamy is flexible. One anthropologist puts it this way: The human mating system "combines short-term and long-term mating bonds, and both types may be overt (known to all group members), or covert (unknown to a majority of group members and disapproved of)." There is an awful lot of joy and heartache hidden in that bloodless description. But whatever we call it, this is the mating system we've got. And, again, exploring how animals deal with the questions of monogamy and good fathering can help us understand something about ourselves; it forces us to acknowledge that we cannot entirely escape our biology.

Birds, including many species besides the emperor penguin, are the best-known example of monogamy among animals and of good fathering. An estimated 92 percent of bird species are monogamous, and nearly the same percentage care for their young, as the husband-and-wife team of David P. Barash, a psychologist, and Judith Eve Lipton, a psychiatrist, report in their book *Strange Bedfellows: The Surprising Connection Between Sex, Evolution and Monogamy*.

But birds might not be quite as monogamous as they seem. Some exercise a bit of the flexibility that humans are known for. An early clue to feathered infidelity arose during the 1970s, when blackbirds were given vasectomies to try to control the population. Yet females mated with vasectomized males laid eggs that hatched. Either the vasectomized blackbirds had grounds to sue for malpractice or something was fishy in birdland. The problem only got worse when modern genetic techniques came along and paternity testing entered the nest. Swans have long been mythologized as a graceful example of harmony and monogamy. That myth toppled when a genetic study of the Australian black swan found that one in six of the young is fathered by a swan other than the father in the nest. It turns out, according to Barash and Lipton, that anywhere between 10 and 40 percent of birds' offspring were the product of liaisons with partners other than the one at the nest.

The attentive behavior of many bird fathers likely dates back to the dinosaurs, birds' ancestors. Several species of dinosaurs, including the oviraptor, a birdlike creature that lived about 75 million years ago, have been found on top of clutches of fossilized eggs. But were these mothers or fathers? Researchers who carefully examined the bones, looking for maternal and reproductive features, believe that these were males—birds' ancestral fathers. Birds learned to be fathers before they learned how to fly.

One reason that mothers contribute as much as they do to their offspring is that they know with certainty that the chicks in the nest or the children in the high chair are theirs. They saw and felt the biological connection with their children at birth. For fathers, there is always some doubt. So they have to calculate the odds. If they're pretty sure the kids are theirs, then it makes evolutionary sense to raise them and keep those genes going. If there is some doubt, it might make sense for a male to seek another female and try again, with perhaps a better chance that he'll be raising his own kids, not somebody else's.

Swans might be fooled about who the fathers are, but

it's harder to fool humans. Men who suspect that the child they're caring for is not theirs are increasingly seeking paternity tests. And according to one report, 30 percent of them are finding out that their suspicions were correct. This is unlikely to be true for the population overall; these were men who already had suspicions. But it's an impressively large number. Nobody can say for sure how many children in the United States are being raised by men who *think* they are the child's father. We might expect that few fathers would volunteer to participate in a study to determine that.

A woman can have only one child a year, but a man can, theoretically, have an almost limitless number—one a year with each female he is able to mate with. This pattern holds in those animals, including humans, in which males are typically larger than females. In these species, males tend to compete for multiple female partners, they tend to be more aggressive, and they have less invested in their children than females do. In humans, the differences between males and females are not as great as they are, say, in elephant seals—whose males keep harems. Most human males don't. In a few bird species, the opposite is true: females have multiple male partners. Humans are closer to the middle of this spectrum. Males are more likely than females to seek out multiple partners, compete with one another, and make a smaller investment in their children. And that's reflected in our conceptions of men and women.

Although we might try to fight the stereotypes, we commonly expect that men are going to be more likely than women to stray from a marriage or to commit indiscretions, even if the marriage endures. As Barash and Lipton point out, a wandering male cannot justify his infidelity by blaming it on his genes; we *are* able to rise above our evolutionary constraints. At the same time, it's not reasonable to expect couples to remain faithful simply because we demand it; they can't completely escape their biology, as our experience— and indeed, all of human history—tells us. Couples don't file for divorce on the grounds that their prehuman ancestors made them do it. They blame their marital dissolution on infidelity or cruelty or desertion. But their ancestors *do* have something to do with it.

Monkeys are more at the mercy of their evolutionary heritage than humans. Still, in the right circumstances they, too, can transcend their genetic predisposition. Experiments have shown that even in species in which fathers have little or nothing to do with their young, males can be coaxed to rise to the challenge of fatherhood. Stephen J. Suomi of the National Institutes of Health has spent his career working with rhesus monkeys. "They are probably one of the worst species to study the effects of fathers," Suomi says. "The females won't let them get near their kids. They chase them away." When rhesus males reach adolescence, they leave the troop they were born in and search for a new one. Then they must compete with the males in the new troop to reproduce. That's the basic social structure. It's easy to see what he means when he says fatherhood isn't important to rhesus monkeys.

But even these monkeys can be good fathers when the opportunity arises. To make the point, Suomi points to a forty-year-old study by William K. Redican at the California Primate Research Center of the University of California, Davis. Redican removed infant rhesus monkeys from their mothers and left them with their fathers. Because fathers can't nurse, Redican hand-fed the infants. He collected data on the fathers and infants for seven months, in the absence of mothers and peers. When they were no longer being chased away by the mothers, the males became remarkably good fathers. They did almost everything the females would do with two exceptions. One, of course, was that the fathers couldn't nurse the infants. The other was that they played with the kids much more than females do. "Mothers don't do much of that," Suomi says.

Redican described the discovery in even more extravagant terms. "One of the most striking aspects of the male-infant interactions thus far has been the remarkable amount of play that has emerged," he wrote. "The frequency and intensity of this play far exceeded our expectations." Male infants played with their fathers more than female infants. And even the style of play was interesting. "After an interval of intense clasping and play-biting, the infant typically began struggling to break away," Redican wrote. It would then run to a far corner of the cage, sometimes making play faces at its father or swatting at him. "Typically the infant then jumped back toward the male, often at his face, and clasping and play-biting resumed." These experiments, along with the many other animal studies, reinforce the notion that biology prepares animals for fatherhood—even when fathers are typically not allowed to act on that impulse, as is the case with the rhesus monkeys. But Redican was impressed by the fathers' flexibility under the artificial circumstances. "We are again reminded of the folly and perhaps arrogance of making sweeping statements about the limits of an animal's behavioral repertoire," Redican concluded.

It's a lesson we might take to heart as we consider human parenting. As with Redican's rhesus fathers, human fathers also demonstrate enormous flexibility. When little help is around, fathers pitch in and take on a much larger share of the work. But what's important to us—what we see in animals and in men—is that males can engage deeply with their offspring. The depth of that engagement can be measured by what happens when it is interrupted. And one way that can happen is when men succumb to postpartum depression, which can pull them away from their emotional connections to their children. Postpartum depression in mothers is something we know about. What's new is the recognition that fathers, too, can suffer from postpartum depression.

This is more common in men that we've recognized. In the postpartum period, one in ten new fathers suffers from moderate to severe depression, a striking increase over the 3 to 5 percent of men in the general population who are depressed. These fathers (like mothers with depression) are less likely than others to read, tell stories, or sing songs to their infants. But according to one study, the infants of depressed fathers, in particular, have a much smaller vocabulary at age two than other children. This link has not been found with depressed mothers. And male postpartum depression has been linked to conduct problems or hyperactivity in their children three years later. Children of fathers who have major depression can be eight times as likely as others to have behavior problems, and thirty-six times as likely as other kids to have difficulties dealing with their peers. What happens to fathers can happen to their children, too.

Lambert's mice, the emperor penguins, and seahorses have each crafted a unique approach to fatherhood. Each of them teaches us something about being a parent, and about our own peculiarities. Most important, studies of animals, monogamy, and depression all demonstrate the close connection between fathers and their children. Of course, carrying our kids around on our backs all day would probably ruin our knees. And our flexible version of monogamy is likely to persist. But we have made progress. Fathers are no longer confined to the waiting room with Ricky Ricardo, and we should be grateful for that. Changes in the workplace mean many fathers now have more opportunity to become involved with their children than they had before, and we should be grateful for that as well. We can't blame our ancestors for our failings, but we might want to thank them for what they've given us: fathers' involvement with their children is an indispensable feature of human existence. And as we will see in the next chapter, preparation that begins before conception, fathers' involvement during pregnancy, and their presence in the delivery room all put fathers in a good position to engage with their infants.

FIVE

Infants: Sculpting Fathers' Brains

I've noted many times—and it will come up again—how often fathers are missing from research on children's development. We see this in laboratories, in discussions about child rearing and parenting, and in the attitudes of the people who stock pediatricians' waiting rooms exclusively with women's magazines. (If you're looking for *Sports Illustrated*, you can find it in the urologist's office.) So I don't want to be accused of the reverse—leaving mothers out of the conversation. And they are relevant here, as we discuss the arrival of a new family member and the beginning of parenthood.

Fathers don't parent alone. Even if they are single fathers, their parenting is shaped by the temperament and reactions of their child and by whether they have one child, two, or a dozen. In two-parent families, the relationship parents have with each other has a lot to do with their relationships with their children. Indeed, many researchers would argue that there is a fundamental error in thinking about fathering or mothering as activities that involve two people—the parent and the child. The reality is that the entire family functions as a unit, and it's difficult to conclude too much from the study of one parent and one child in isolation.

For years, researchers studied parenting in terms of what they called these "dyadic" relationships. And most often the crucial dyad was believed to be the mother and child, leaving the father out altogether. One of the thinkers who began to change that was Salvador Minuchin, whose book *Families and Family Therapy*, published in 1974, was one of the first to propose looking at the family as an intricate system, in which each part affects all the others. Examining the carburetor, the exhaust pipes, or the engine block tells us little about what makes a car go, unless we consider all of them together, along with the transmission, the driveshaft, and all the rest. The same kind of thing, Minuchin argued, is true of families. He cared little, for example, about the specifics of who did the diapering, who washed the dishes, and who handled the discipline in a family. What was crucial was that the family system *worked*—and that the parents had forged an alliance with each other.

That's not to say that working out the details of family duties isn't important; it is. But what's of primary importance is that parents have a plan, with shared goals and a division of chores that suits them. Whether two parents divide the responsibility for changing diapers fifty-fifty isn't important in itself, unless one parent feels unfairly burdened and becomes frustrated and angry. What's important in that case is that they haven't agreed on a plan—not just that somebody is getting stuck with too many diapers.

Another way to think of the family "system" comes from the late psychologist Urie Bronfenbrenner, whose book *The Ecology of Human Development* suggests that families should be thought of as little ecosystems, in which the parts are as interdependent as the insects, plants, fish, trees, and birds in and around a pond. Bronfenbrenner's book, like Minuchin's, was published in the 1970s, around the time that Michael Lamb was beginning his research on fathers, inaugurating the boom in father research that was to come over the next few decades.

The family system, however, does not always run smoothly. Before couples become parents, they can't always anticipate how different the situation will be once their child arrives. In their studies of new parents, Philip and Carolyn Cowan, the researchers whose own marriage was threatened by the arrival of children, asked expectant fathers and mothers to think about various roles in their lives—worker, friend, mother, daughter, father, and so on— and to mark them on a pie chart according to which felt most important, not how much time each one demanded. Mothers marked far larger portions for motherhood than fathers did for fatherhood. In late pregnancy, mothers already said, on average, that motherhood made up 10 percent of their lives—twice as much as what fathers said about fatherhood.

This was in the 1980s, and parents might fill out those pie charts a bit differently now. But what is interesting about this is not so much what the pie charts said, but how they changed after the birth of a child. Once the couples had become parents, both mothers and fathers, when asked to fill out another pie chart, increased the portion devoted to parenthood, although fathers' wedges were still less than one-third as large as those of their partners. Oddly, however, men who gave fatherhood larger pieces of pie had higher self-esteem when their babies were six months old— while women who gave motherhood larger shares of their lives tended to have lower self-esteem. "It looks like new fathers who feel good about themselves are able to devote more energy to their parent identity without giving up other central aspects of their psychological lives," the Cowans concluded. "And what they get back from this relationship helps them to keep their self-esteem on a positive track."

Women did not get the same bounce. When the babies of the couples in the study were six months old, women gave work an 18 percent share of their pies. Men gave it 28 percent. Even for women who worked full-time, "mother" took up 50 percent more of the pie than "worker." Fathers' pie charts were dramatically different. Their estimate of the portion of their lives devoted to work didn't change, and fatherhood always took up a smaller share of their pies than work. Being a good father clearly had rewards for men that were different from what women got from being good mothers.

Interestingly, the share of the pies allocated to "partner" dropped for both men and women, as you might expect—from 34 percent during pregnancy for women to 22 percent when their children were six months old; and from 35 percent to 30 percent for men. But significantly, the parents with the highest estimates of their partnering share had the highest self-esteem and the lowest parental stress.

The Cowans were among the first to pay so much attention to fathers. They were still operating in the shadow of John Bowlby's attachment theory, which we've already encountered. Bowlby thought fathers weren't capable of the kind of attachment that mothers and infants experienced with one another. Nobody, including Bowlby, had found evidence that fathers were unimportant during infancy. The problem was that nobody had done the research to find out.

One of the first to question attachment theory and its dismissal of fathers was Milton Kotelchuck, a Harvard psychologist. "What hard evidence is there to support the notion that children relate uniquely to their mothers?" Kotelchuck asked in the 1970s. It was a radical question at a time when most psychiatrists and psychologists still clung to the idea that fathers didn't matter, or didn't matter much.

Kotelchuck did four studies using what's called the strange situation experiment—a psychological tool devised by Mary Ainsworth to assess attachment. It's ordinarily done by observing a child, its mother, and a stranger interacting as the adults enter and leave a room. In a typical setup, the child refuses to be comforted by a stranger when the mother leaves, but stops crying almost immediately when the mother returns—demonstrating the child's attachment to the mother. Kotelchuck simply added a father to the cast of characters entering and leaving. He then recorded what happened with different combinations of adults in the room. Babies consistently stayed close to their parents, initiated interaction with them, smiled and vocalized to both mother and father—and stayed away from the strangers. The infants didn't protest the departure of a strange female, but they did protest the departure of each parent. "Both the mother and father served extensively as bases of security and interaction for the child," Kotelchuck wrote.

But there were differences. About half of the infants showed a preference for mother over father. Another quarter of them showed a preference for their fathers, and most of the rest showed equal preference for both. The findings were the same whether the infants were girls or boys.

When Kotelchuck interviewed the parents after the sessions, he asked how they shared child care at home. He was surprised to discover that only 25 percent of these middle-class Boston fathers had regular daily responsibility for their kids. Nearly half had never changed a diaper. There was a telling link between the experimental data and the information on home care, however: those infants who didn't seem to relate to their fathers in the strange situation experiment came from the families reporting the least amount of child care delivered by the father.

When Michael Lamb began his research just after Kotelchuck's, he used a different strategy. He ditched the strange situation experiment and looked at how infants behaved in their homes when they were distressed and wanted to be held. As most parents know, infants don't generally like to be held or comforted by others—even friends—when people they're attached to are around. Lamb chose ten infant girls and ten boys and observed them in their homes, with both parents present, when the children were seven months old and then again at eight months. Each observation lasted about two hours.

He found that fathers and mothers both played with the infants about the same amount of time, but infants responded more positively to the fathers. And fathers tended to be more physical and idiosyncratic with their games. Mothers held infants much more than fathers did, but fathers were more likely to play with children when they picked them up. Infants clearly recognized the difference—even though the difference between the children's reactions to their mothers and to their fathers was not anywhere near as stark as attachment theory would have predicted.

More recent studies have broadened understanding of

the close links between fathers and infants first found by Lamb. Fathers, like mothers, quickly recognize the unique qualities of their own children by touch, even when they can't see or smell them. Men who were exposed to their new-born children for only sixty minutes were able to recognize their own infants merely by touching their hands. Mothers, who had spent more time with the babies before testing, were also able to recognize their newborns by their faces, but both mothers and fathers did best by touching the new-borns' hands.

Lamb and his successors were finally demonstrating in the lab what many of us instinctively know: that fathers of-ten show the same elation as mothers when their children are born and the same anxiety about leaving them, and are similarly nurturing and attentive. Fathers also pick up on cues that their infants are hungry, and they engage in baby talk, speaking slowly and repeating themselves.

But fathers, as we've seen, do differ from mothers in some respects. For one thing, they have a unique response to their babies' cries. This is being investigated by James E. Swain, a child and adolescent psychiatrist and neuroscien-tist at the University of Michigan. He began his research with mothers, putting them in fMRI machines (short for functional magnetic resonance imaging) to scan their brains and find out what happened when they heard infants cry. The fMRI scanners are capable of picking up activity in dif-ferent regions of the brain. Swain wanted to know if the brain's response to an infant's cry differed from its response to a similarly unpleasant sound that didn't come from an infant, and whether a mother's response to her own child's cry differed from the response to an unrelated child's cry. This was one way to measure the mother's empathy for her child—especially important with infants, who have important needs that they make clear mostly by nonverbal communication.

He began by scanning the brains of first-time mothers while they listened to thirty seconds of their own infants' crying, compared to thirty seconds of other sounds with similar patterns and intensity. And the scans were done on the mothers twice—first at two to four weeks after their children were born, and again at twelve to sixteen weeks postpartum. Then he repeated the scans with fathers.

Swain found substantial differences in the way parents' brains responded to their own infants' cries versus those of other infants. Many parents say they can walk into a day care center with dozens of children and pick out their own baby's cry. The work provided some scientific validation for that claim. While mothers showed greater activation in some brain regions than fathers, both showed positive responses to their own babies.

I met Swain at his office in Ann Arbor, on the University of Michigan's corporate-style North Campus. Swain, who said he is not a father but has recently married "and might become one," has long been interested in human growth and development, and how animals, including humans, develop from their earliest moments. Such things can be tricky to study, particularly because it's often hard to know whether children's behavior is the result of their genes, their environment, or both.

Swain recalled an earlier case in which researchers had been fooled. They were doing studies of rats that showed that mothers who frequently licked their pups gave birth to pups who grew up to do the same to their offspring. Likewise, mothers who were "low lickers" passed that quality on to their offspring. "Everyone guessed it was genetic," Swain said. The story was almost too good to be true. These findings were appearing at a time when researchers were discarding Freud's notion that infant and childhood relationships were overwhelmingly responsible for the kinds of adults that children turned out to be. Now it looked as if genes were the prime influence on developing animals, including children.

But that explanation quickly evaporated when researchers tried a different experiment: "They switched the pups," Swain said. Offspring of high lickers were given to low-licking mothers, and vice versa. It was immediately clear that genetics was *not* responsible for the difference. "The environment predicted their behavior, not the background genetics," Swain said. The offspring acquired the behavior of their adoptive parents, not their biological parents. And there was more. "Through some magical process, the licking and grooming alters the expression of cortisol receptors in the hippocampus. The genes that regulate the expression of these stress receptors are altered, so those pups that were licked a lot are less sensitive to stress." Licking was capable of actually changing the pups' brains. This was an important reminder that genetics is only part of what makes a good father.

After he finished medical school, Swain moved to Yale to study with James F. Leckman, an authority on obsessive-compulsive disorder. Leckman was pursuing the idea that parenting could be thought of as a particular kind of obsessive-compulsive behavior. People with obsessive-compulsive disorder sometimes wash their hands endlessly or check the door dozens of times to be sure it's locked, along with other repetitive behaviors. I asked Swain whether a similar thing was happening to me when I would sometimes check my sleeping infants every ten minutes to make sure they were breathing. He told me that a little parental obsession and compulsion in the days and weeks after a child's birth could actually boost a child's chances of survival. So I wasn't crazy (well, not entirely), and my personal obsessions were, at least partly, a good thing. I stopped obsessing over my obsession. I hope I can one day do the same with respect to the viselike grip I apply to my children's arms when we're crossing the street.

Leckman took this idea of parenting as obsession seriously enough to do a study of obsessions in parents. He and his colleagues recruited forty-one couples and interviewed them before the birth of their children, two weeks after the births, and again at three months. They were asked about such things as their thoughts about the baby's well-being and growth; the number of times they checked on the baby, changed diapers, and comforted him or her; their thoughts about the baby's future and about being a parent; the number of times they played with or talked to the baby; and their worries, anxiety, and their partner's health.

It will come as little surprise that parents were indeed preoccupied by their children. Mothers reported thinking about the baby an average of fourteen hours per day and fathers seven hours per day. This preoccupation, as the researchers had predicted, peaked about two weeks after birth and subsided by three months after their children's births. The effect was strongest in mothers—but significant in fathers as well. Fathers showed a more striking increase in preoccupation from the eighth month of pregnancy to the time of birth. The birth of a child is "associated with an altered mental state for both parents . . . a time of heightened sensitivity and preoccupation. It is a time of increased responsibility, and a time when things need to be as perfect as possible." Before birth, "parents routinely experience intrusive thoughts and images of physical malformations, mental retardation, and possible health problems . . . After birth this landscape of worry shifts to frightening images and thoughts of dropping the infant, the infant being attacked by pets or stray animals, the infant being injured or sickened because of the parents' inability to recognize a problem or because of their negligence."

I'm afraid I didn't need Leckman's research to be persuaded that these "intrusive thoughts" can be a problem. I experience them often, and I can report that they can be disturbing and unpleasant. But I take comfort from his idea that this behavior evolved to ensure children's survival. During our history as a species, deaths of infants and children were far more common than they are now. It's only in the past few centuries that health care, food safety, and changes in our living arrangements have combined to push infant mortality rates below 1 percent. The intrusive thoughts that some of us experience might now have outlived their usefulness, but they were important once. And they might be still. Anxiety in new parents and obsessive-compulsive disorder do indeed resemble each other. The difference is that symptoms that can be devastating to a person with obsessive-compulsive disorder can be useful—up to a point— when caring for a new infant. I've often joked with my wife that our anxiety about the kids is a special kind of temporary insanity. Or perhaps not so temporary. Three of my children are grown, and while I'm now less likely to wake up at 3:00 a.m. worrying about them, I can't say my anxiety has completely disappeared.

Leckman's work with parental obsessions led to Swain's research, first on mothers and then on fathers. Some of his experiments produced interesting and controversial findings. One study found that breast-feeding mothers showed greater brain response to their babies' cries, compared to the mothers who fed their children formula. Another concluded that birth by cesarean section also affected the way a mother responded to her infant. Mothers who delivered vaginally "were significantly more responsive" to their own babies' cry than mothers who had had cesarean sections.

On the paternal side of the equation, Swain is particularly interested in possible changes in fathers' brains that might reflect sensitive behavior toward infants in the period from two weeks until about four months after birth. Such changes had been shown in mothers, but nobody had looked at fathers. Swain recruited sixteen fathers and assessed their relationship to their infants with a questionnaire that asked how they thought about their infants and how preoccupied they were with them. Swain also observed the fathers with their infants.

When he scanned their brains, he found significant changes during those first four months that paralleled those seen in mothers, including increased activity in the prefrontal cortex in response to looking at pictures of their infants or hearing their cries. It's a striking finding: fathers' brains are being sculpted and shaped by their experience of their children. And these are not random brain changes; the areas that increased in activity seemed to be associated with fathers' motivations and moods, and their involvement with their babies.

Swain is now trying to identify the brain's wiring diagram for these changes. "We're interested in basic cry-response circuitry as well as what changes over time," Swain said. "We're still trying to pull down what is common and what is different about mothers and fathers. There are two areas that come up as common, and they both have their interesting aspects. The insula is a big way station for emotional information, and it looks like there is a direct relationship between own- versus other-baby cry and levels of parental caring thoughts, for both mothers *and* fathers."

Beginning right after birth, mothers show activity in deeper brain structures related to pain and emotion. While fathers show similar activity in the cortex, they don't show this other activity when tested at two to four weeks after their infant's birth. "It might explain why it's easier for the father to roll over when the baby cries at night," Swain said. And it might also explain why mothers are at so much greater risk for postpartum depression, compared to fathers. But at three to four months after birth, when fathers were tested again, their brains "are lighting up in their auditory cortex and these deeper brain areas, but in a complicated pattern. It's not the same as mothers." Fathers are clearly wired to respond to their children; their brains are engaged

Another way of looking for connections between parents and their infants is through the study of a phenomenon known as synchrony. It refers to mothers' ability to match and encourage infants' positive emotions when the two are face-to-face. If baby is happy, mother is happy, and vice versa. The psychologist Ruth Feldman at Bar-Ilan University in Israel, a former colleague of Swain's at Yale, says it is well recognized that mothers can cycle through a range of behaviors with their infants, falling into rhythm with the baby's nursing, crying, or kicking. "Such rhythms are intimately familiar to mothers, who were thus considered biologically equipped to match microlevel shifts in infant affect," Feldman says. But it wasn't known whether fathers were capable of entering this face-to-face "dance" with their infants, despite its obvious importance. Feldman decided to find out.

She enlisted one hundred Israeli couples with five-month-old infants to participate in her study. Each family was videotaped three times at home—once with only mother and infant, once with father and infant, and once with the whole family. Not surprisingly, fathers and mothers engaged their infants' emotions in different ways.

The study showed that mothers and fathers were equally capable of matching their emotions to those of their infants, but each parent offered different experiences to their child. In addition, the degree to which parents and infants synchronized their emotions was greater between mothers and daughters and between fathers and sons.

The emotional pattern in mother-infant interactions ranged from low to medium intensity, and it depended upon the pair gazing into each other's eyes and sharing facial and vocal expressions. The pattern between fathers and infants was much more intense, with sudden peaks that became more common as play progressed. Feldman found that the emotional connections between both parents and their infants could influence the kinds of relationships the children had with others much later in their lives. "Fathers and mothers are equally capable of engaging in second-by-second synchrony with their infant . . . mothers are not unique," she wrote. Father-son pairs showed the highest synchrony, and it revolved around intense emotional peaks related to play.

All of this suggests two things. Fathers clearly have important connections with their infants; and they treat infants differently than mothers do. Evidence for this keeps accumulating, and it underscores the importance of fathers spending both quality and quantity time with their young babies. We now know that men who take time off from work after the birth of their infants are more involved with them later on—which is in turn related to more positive evaluations at work. Everybody wins—fathers, kids, and employers.

But what happens in families in which paternal leave is irrelevant, because the father doesn't have a job? Natasha J. Cabrera of the University of Maryland wanted to know if relationships between fathers and infants would be different in poor and disadvantaged families—sometimes referred to as fragile families. She looked for the answer in data from the Fragile Families and Child Wellbeing Study, a collaboration between Princeton and Columbia Universities to follow 5,000 children born in large American cities between 1998 and 2000. About three-fourths of the children in this study were born to unmarried parents. Cabrera and her colleagues found that fathers who were emotionally engaged with their partners before their children were born were more likely to be involved with the children a year later and three years later. It was an intriguing and useful discovery, because it offered an opportunity to help fragile families. If fathers could be encouraged to get involved during pregnancy, they had a good chance of staying involved with their kids after their birth. Fathers should establish relationships with their children before they are born.

•

Many of these discoveries about fathers and fatherhood have encouraged others to study fathers, and we're getting new insights into fatherhood all the time. One important insight came from a group of Israeli researchers who looked at the involvement of mothers and fathers in caregiving with an emphasis on nighttime behavior, just as Barry Hewlett had done, staying up late to observe Aka fathers at night. For many fathers, bedtime is when they get home from work, and a prime opportunity to spend time with their children. Specifically, the researchers wanted to know if fathers' involvement had any link to sleep patterns. Plenty of studies had linked parenting and infants' sleep, but most of them focused on mothers.

So the researchers recruited fifty-six couples during their first pregnancy, and gave them questionnaires one month and six months after their babies were born. They also assessed infants' sleep with monitors attached to the children to record movement and sleep diaries kept by their parents. (They did not control for any kind of sleep training the parents might have used.)

Mothers, they found, were more involved than fathers in both daytime and nighttime care. But higher father involvement in overall care was associated with fewer nighttime awakenings by their babies. "To our knowledge, this is the first study that assessed how paternal involvement in infant care is related to infant sleep," the researchers wrote.

Another question was whether fathers have a unique influence on behavioral problems in their children. Paul G. Ramchandani of the University of Oxford was one of the first to look at this. His idea was that children whose fathers were more engaged with them, and more sensitive and responsive, would engage in fewer so-called externalizing behaviors, which can include tantrums, biting, and kicking. This behavior is normal for many kids from about twelve months of age until the end of their second year, when it begins to subside. But in about 6 percent of children, it continues, and can last throughout childhood. Children exhibiting the highest levels of these behaviors as preschoolers have shown higher levels of oppositional behavior as adults. The persistence of these externalizing behaviors can have lifelong consequences.

Looking at mostly middle-class families whom they met at home when their infants were three months old and again at one year, the researchers found that more remote father-infant interactions were associated with a higher rate of aggressive behavior in the children. The effects were greater for male infants than for girls. And that held true regardless of how mothers behaved with the infants.

Now we know that fathers can establish a relationship with their children even before they are born and can influence them in many ways—from their sleep patterns to their long-term behavior. And we know that children can help sculpt their fathers' brains. But what else? Are there other ways in which babies shape their fathers?

One way to answer this question is to look at men's testosterone levels. In many animals, including humans, testosterone levels are low following the arrival of a newborn. But it's unclear what that means. It could be that fatherhood leads to a drop in testosterone. Or alternatively, the explanation might be that men with lower testosterone levels are the ones that choose to become fathers. Which comes first, the baby or the plummeting testosterone?

To find out, Lee T. Gettler and Christopher W. Kuzawa of Northwestern University looked at 624 men in Cebu, the oldest city in the Philippines, where fathers are commonly involved in day-to-day care of their children. The researchers collected saliva samples to measure testosterone when the men were twenty-one years old and again when they were twenty-six.

Gettler and Kuzawa predicted that men with higher testosterone would have greater success at finding a mate and becoming a father. They expected that these men would show the greatest decrease in testosterone when they became fathers, and that those who spent more time taking care of their children would have lower levels of testosterone. In other words, marrying, having children, and taking care of them would all lower a man's testosterone—and the effect would be greatest in those who had the highest testosterone to start with. And that's what they found. (Even sleeping with children can affect testosterone levels in fathers. An extraordinarily high 92 percent of 362 Philippine fathers in Cebu reported "cosleeping" in the same bed as their children. They showed a significant decline in testosterone compared to fathers who slept in a different room.)

The modulation of testosterone that comes with partnering and fatherhood might also be good for men's health. Fathers who are involved with their children have a reduced risk of illness and mortality that might be explained by their lower testosterone levels. High testosterone may increase the risk of prostate cancer and unhealthy cholesterol levels. And it's been linked to risk-taking that can affect men's health, such as drug and alcohol use and promiscuity. Despite these well-known consequences of high testosterone, drug makers are promoting testosterone creams and gels that can boost testosterone levels. Fathers who have close relationships with their children, and whose testosterone has fallen as a result, are now a profit center for the pharmaceutical industry. Ironically, the use of topical testosterone can be dangerous to children who come into contact with it. The cream or gel, on a father's hands or on his body, can cause enlargement of children's sex organs, premature development of pubic hair, and aggressive behavior. Fathers might be wiser to enjoy their children and let their testosterone levels fall where they may.

But it's not that simple. In a small, early effort to explore the biology behind father-infant attachments, Karen M. Grewen of the University of North Carolina and her then-student Patty X. Kuo videotaped ten men while they were spending time with their infants, and took testosterone samples at the same time. They also put the men in brain scanners while they watched video of their own or other children. The scans showed greater prefrontal and subcortical activity in men watching videotapes of any infant compared to video of a doll. Video images of their own children produced greater activity than images of just any child. And testosterone levels correlated with brain activity: happy infants' faces produced activity in the left caudate, a "reward" region of fathers' brains, and fathers who responded strongly in this region to the sight of their own infants also experienced a rise in testosterone.

It's a bit of a paradox. Low testosterone seems to be connected with good fathering, but testosterone might rise in response to signals such as crying and could be linked to a father's protective response toward his infant. Attachment is clearly part of a complicated system; there is no simple link between the way testosterone varies and the kind of fathers men turn out to be. But brain activity, hormones, and behavior are all closely linked. And fathering clearly is a deeply ingrained behavior.

One night when one of my younger children was old enough to sit up but still a baby, he awoke in the middle of the night crying. My wife fed him, and we tried to console him. He finally settled down, but then we had another problem. It was three or four in the morning, as I recall, but on his internal clock, it was high noon. He was ready to play.

It's a scenario many parents are familiar with, and it always seems to happen the night before an important meeting or a deadline. I had the feeling I hadn't quite been doing my share on the night shift, so I volunteered to stay up with him. And I remembered doing this with my older children. You stay up and read stories or tickle or wrestle, all the time looking for the droopy eyes that mean you might be able to get him to slip off to sleep—and salvage something of your own night.

This is the kind of thing I remember about having an infant in the house. These sleepless nights seem as though they will never end, until, without warning, they do. The kids grow up and find other ways to console themselves in the middle of the night. So I decided I would enjoy our time on the night shift together. The research on the connections between fathers and infants is catching up with the experiences many of us have had with our own children. It's nice to know that these feelings of attachment, for so long denied by orthodox psychologists, are not some delusion, but are supported by the facts.

I don't remember what happened at work the day after that sleepless night—whether I was tired or missed a meeting. But I remember the hours with my son.

SIX

Children: Language, Learning, and *Batman*

From World War II through the 1960s, the few experts who thought about fathers believed that their main contribution was to be role models for gender-appropriate behavior by their sons. They were supposed to teach their sons what it meant to be a man, as they usually put it. A few researchers thought it might be nice to measure that effect to see whether there was truly a correlation between masculinity in fathers and masculinity in their sons. (Masculinity refers to what we traditionally think of as male characteristics: toughness, power, status, sturdiness in a crisis, a willingness to take risks and to ignore what others think.) The link should have been easy to find, but it wasn't. There was no consistent connection between a father's masculinity and his son's. This posed a challenge to the conventional wisdom. If fathers weren't helping to make boys into men, then what role did they have?

The problem was that nobody had asked *why* boys might want to be like their fathers. Presumably they would want to emulate their fathers only if they liked and respected them and had warm relationships with them. When researchers decided to look for that, in the 1960s, they discovered that the relationship between father and son was crucially important. When a father had a warm relationship with his son, that son would grow up to be more like his father than sons who were not close to their fathers. A father's own masculinity was irrelevant; his warmth and closeness with his son was the key factor.

This was one of the first indications that fathers have a particularly strong influence on children's social development. Interactions between fathers and their sons and daughters that are playful, affectionate, and engaging predict later popularity in school and among peers, perhaps by teaching children to read emotional expressions on their fathers' faces, and later on those of their peer group. Harsh discipline by fathers, on the other hand, has been linked to later behavior problems in their kids.

These early discoveries prompted careful examination of fathers and their influence on their toddlers and school-age children. And one of the areas in which researchers looked for the influence of fathers was in the development of language. I've always thought that watching children learn to talk is one of the highlights of parenting. It's a hallmark of their lives during their first few years. They learn to make their wishes known—often *emphatically* known. What begins in infancy with gestures and sounds develops into competence with language by around age three. Fathers are proving to be an important part of this process, as Lynne Vernon-Feagans of the University of North Carolina and her colleague Nadya Pancsofar at the College of New Jersey are finding out.

They have done some of the most interesting work looking at children's language development in both middle-class and poor, rural families. They've found, to their surprise, that not only are fathers important for children's language development, but that fathers matter *more* than mothers. In middle-class families, parents' overall level of education and the quality of child care were both related to children's language development. But fathers "made unique contributions to children's expressive language development" that went "above and beyond" the contributions of education and child care. When fathers used more words with their children during play, children had more advanced language skills a year later. The implication is that fathers may also be making important contributions to their children's later success in school.

Vernon-Feagans and Pancsofar suspected the situation might be different in poor families, so they decided to take a look. They selected families from central Pennsylvania and eastern North Carolina, where about half of children lived in poverty at the time. A total of 1,292 infants in two-parent families participated in the study. The researchers visited the children's families when the children were six months old, fifteen months old, and three years old. They found that fathers' education and their use of vocabulary when reading picture books to their children at six months of age were significantly related to the children's expressiveness at fifteen months and use of advanced language at age three. This held true no matter what the mother's educational level was or how she spoke to the children.

When I spoke with Vernon-Feagans about her findings, she said she was surprised by the difference between mothers and fathers. She had thought they would be equally involved in encouraging their children's language development. Why would fathers be more important in this regard than mothers? The hypothesis is that it's because mothers are more attuned to their children, typically spending more time with them than fathers do. That makes mothers more likely to choose words the kids are familiar with. Fathers aren't as attuned to their kids, so they use a broader vocabulary, and their children learn new words and concepts as a result.

Vernon-Feagans thought there might be another factor at play as well. Because fathers usually spend less time with their children, they are more of a novelty. That makes them more interesting playmates. When she looked at the videos from her language experiments, she saw that fathers were very engaged. Playing with their children was something they enjoyed. It didn't matter what their income was. "I do think our children see it as very special when they do book reading with their fathers . . . They may listen more and acquire language in a special way." The effect of fathers on children's language continues until they enter school.

But fathers contribute to their children's mental development more broadly than just with respect to language. They also influence their children's intellectual growth, adjustment to school, and behavior, as Catherine Tamis-LeMonda of New York University and her colleagues discovered. They were interested in the influence of fathers on language in families involved in Head Start, a federal program intended to enhance the intellectual, emotional, and social development of low-income children in the years before they start school. According to the researchers, poor fathers can have difficulty maintaining "positive and emotionally supportive relationships with their children," in part because they have limited resources and often unstable employment. Tamis-LeMonda and her colleagues studied 290 fathers who lived in the home with their children and their partners, to find out how their play with children differed from that of mothers, and how their behavior related to their children's language and cognitive development. The researchers watched fathers' interactions with their children—and, separately, mothers' interactions with their children—during a period of free play when the children were two years old, and again when they were three. They found that these were mostly good parents. They challenged the assumption by some researchers "that low-income parents primarily engage in authoritarian exchanges with their young children and that fathers are harsh disciplinarians." And the sensitivity of the parents, their positive regard for their children, and the intellectual stimulation they offered predicted that the children would do well on tests of development and vocabulary later on.

Supportive parenting on the part of fathers was linked to a boost in children's intellectual development and their language abilities. Fathers' good behavior also improved the behavior of mothers with their children—an interesting indirect effect of good fathering. But the importance of father's income varies from one study to the next. Daniel Nettle of Newcastle University found that wealthier fathers produced a greater rise in their children's IQs than did similarly active low-income fathers. Nettle doesn't say why this income disparity exists. It might sound discouraging, but it suggests that improving men's educational or financial status would confer benefits not only on them but on their children as well.

But that's not to say that fathers in poorer families have no influence; they do. In 2011, Erin Pougnet, Alex E. Schwartzman, and their colleagues at Concordia University in

Montreal set out to assess fathers' influence over children's intellectual development and behavioral problems by looking at lower- to middle-income families in which the fathers lived apart from their children, which is the case in about 22 percent of Quebec families. These families have reduced incomes, and the children are less likely to graduate from high school. The researchers looked at the data on the children when they were three to five years old, and again when they were nine to thirteen years old. They found that the presence of fathers in the home was associated with fewer of what are called "internalizing" problems—depression, fear, and self-doubt—in their daughters . . . but not in their sons. It was unclear why that was the case. And the children of fathers who exhibited more positive kinds of control, such as reasoning, scored higher on a measure of nonverbal intelligence called performance IQ.

How fathers exert these effects is still being teased out. But clearly one way they do it is, again, through play. Mothers, who generally spend more time with their children, are seen by their kids as crucial sources of well-being and security. Children are more likely to think of their fathers as playmates. So it's not too surprising that infants respond more positively to being picked up by their fathers, because they suspect that means it's playtime.

"Fathers often use objects in an incongruous way," writes Daniel Paquette of the University of Montreal. During rough-and-tumble play like this, fathers tend to use playful teasing to "destabilize children both emotionally and cognitively," which children like—despite the seemingly ominous implications of the word "destabilizing." It might not sound like a good idea, but this destabilization could have a critical function. It could be helping our children confront one of their principal challenges: the need to learn how to deal with unexpected events. Children's need to be "stimulated, pushed and encouraged to take risks is as great as their need for stability and security," says Paquette.

He describes fathers as having an "activation relationship" with their children that "fosters children's opening to the world." Fathers' unpredictability helps children learn to be brave in difficult situations or when meeting new people. In one study of one-year-olds taken to swimming class, researchers observed that fathers were more likely to stand behind their children, so that the children faced the water, while mothers tended to stand in front of the children, the better to make eye contact. In another study, Paquette used the strange situation experiment pioneered by Ainsworth in her research on attachment. He would have a strange adult enter an unfamiliar room with a child, or put toys at the top of a staircase so a toddler would have to climb to get them. Paquette found that fathers were more likely than mothers to encourage risk-taking by being less protective, especially with their sons. He concluded that fathers may be especially important in supporting their children as they move from the family to the world outside the door. And one of the first and most important unfamiliar environments that children encounter is school. Children who make the transition from home to school more easily, who are free of behavior problems and relate well to their peers and teachers, are more likely to do well in kindergarten and elementary school.

Researchers at the National Institute of Child Health and Human Development wanted to know how parenting behavior and beliefs are related to children's transition to school. Much of the previous research had looked at whether fathers were present or absent in the home, and those studies found that the presence of fathers was associated with better outcomes for children. That wasn't terribly surprising. But the researchers went further, to find out why that mattered. They found that when fathers showed sensitivity to their child in the transition to school and encouraged their child's autonomy, it predicted a much better relationship between the child and his or her teacher. Paternal encouragement was also associated with better behavior and good social skills on the part of the child.

One of the most convincing summaries of fathers' contribution to children's development comes from Sweden. Researchers at Uppsala University wanted to know if there was evidence to support arguments for more parental leave for fathers and for other measures that would increase the involvement of fathers in child rearing. They collected twenty-four of what they thought were the best studies of father involvement and children's outcomes. The studies were longitudinal, meaning they followed fathers and their families over at least a year. Such studies are generally more persuasive than those that simply ask families about current or past practices in the home. And when the data from a number of studies is combined and analyzed together in what's called a meta-analysis, it can sometimes produce clearer results than can any single study alone.

The researchers found a wide variety of beneficial social and psychological effects stemming from fathers' direct engagement with their children. Children whose fathers played with them, read to them, took them on outings, and helped care for them had fewer behavioral problems in the early school years, and less likelihood of delinquency or criminal behavior as adolescents.

Among disadvantaged children born prematurely, those with engaged fathers had higher IQs at age three than those children whose fathers had not been playing with them or helping to care for them. Children with involved fathers were less likely to smoke as teenagers. And here was a particularly stunning result: fathers reading to seven-year-old girls and asking sixteen-year-old girls about school helped to prevent depression and other psychological ailments in the kids decades later. The researchers' conclusion? Enough is now known about the positive impact of fathers' presence on children's lives that governments should start changing public policies to encourage fathers to spend time with their children.

Fathers' importance in children's transition to school, and their establishment of new relationships and friendships, was also explored by Ross D. Parke of the University of California, Riverside, who has focused largely on the social development of children. He believes that fathers play a central role in children's socialization. In a 2004 study, Parke and his colleagues note that this key aspect of children's development is linked to a network of relationships inside and outside the family. Fathers and mothers both influence children's peer relationships, sometimes in overlapping ways. And children will be influenced by their peers, with whom they can have many different kinds of relationships. We want our children to be socially adept and well adjusted, and understanding how they form peer relationships can help us help them become more comfortable socially.

As far back as World War II, researchers noticed that U.S. children whose fathers were away at war when their children were four to eight years old later had problems with peer relationships. The same was true for the sons of Norwegian sailors, who were away for months at a time. Their fathers were not there to help them learn how to behave with others, and the children were consequently less popular and (hardly surprisingly) less satisfied with their relationships with their friends. In a separate study, one group of researchers watched fathers in their homes playing with their three- and four-year-old children. Teachers were then asked to rank the children according to their popularity among their classmates in preschool. Children of fathers who engaged in the most physical and enjoyable play had the highest popularity ratings.

Much of the evidence linking fathers to their children's social competence comes back to the way they play with their children. You might notice a recurring theme here. Play changes as children grow older; tickling and chasing toddlers is gradually replaced by teaching kids to ride a bicycle, playing catch, riding roller coasters, and other more sophisticated kinds of play. (In my case, when my kids were teenagers and ready for Batman: The Ride at Six Flags, I was too terrified to join them. I still feel bad about that.) Play changes, but it remains a central part of the interactions between children and their fathers throughout childhood.

Ross Parke thinks the *way* a father plays is the key to healthy development in kids. He says that when fathers exert too much control over the play, instead of responding to their children's cues, their sons can have more difficulty with their peers. Daughters who were the most popular likewise enjoyed playing with their fathers and had the most "nondirective" fathers. The children of these fathers also tended to have easier transitions into elementary school.

Children whose fathers took turns being the one to suggest activities and showed an interest in the child's suggestions grew up to be less aggressive, more competent, and better liked. These were fathers who played actively with their children, but were not authoritarian; father and child engaged in give-and-take.

The importance of play might be connected to the demands it places on both fathers and children to recognize one another's emotional signals during fast-paced, intense activity—which is what children also need to do with their peers. Fathers who've said they remember both the good and bad in their own childhoods are more likely to be sensitive to the needs and feelings of their children.

Before we get too carried away with the joys of fatherhood, we should note that there is a dark side, too. The connection between fathers and their children can have disturbing consequences for kids, sometimes in unexpected ways. One example concerns children's weight. In 2012, researchers from the University of Adelaide in Australia examined data on the families of 134 nine-year-old Australian children, nearly a quarter of whom were overweight or obese. The researchers found no association between the mothers' work schedules and their children's weight, contradicting some earlier research.

Fathers' work schedules were, in contrast, significantly associated with an increased likelihood that their children would be overweight or obese. And that was true whether or not the mothers worked long or odd hours. The reason, they speculate, is that the fathers' complicated schedules put extra time pressure on families, meaning children were more likely to get quick meals high in fat, sugar, and salt. The effect was important enough that the researchers concluded that any program designed to help overweight or obese children should consider fathers' work schedules.

Another example of fathers' behavior that can be harmful to children is smoking. We know that secondhand smoke poses all sorts of health risks to adults as well as children. Mothers' smoking during pregnancy is associated with a variety of health risks, including her infant's future mental health—specifically in terms of acting out, which can impair the child's ability to participate in social activities and make friends. But up until now, evidence linking fathers' smoking to fetal harm has been less clear. Fathers' smoking has been associated with overweight children, but most of those studies looked at families in lower socioeconomic brackets, in which other factors could have explained the children's obesity.

To determine the consequences of fathers' smoking on children, researchers analyzed data on more than six thousand children in Hong Kong, where smoking is not confined to those in lower economic brackets and where most smokers are men. The children were assessed when they were seven years old and again when they were eleven. Those whose fathers smoked when the mothers were pregnant were more likely to be overweight or obese. It was the first evidence supporting the idea that childhood obesity could be affected by a mother's exposure to her husband's smoking while she was pregnant.

When we add up everything we know about fathers and children, we find overwhelming evidence that engaged fathers contribute to better outcomes for their toddlers and school-age children in a variety of ways. During the course of my interviews, however, I came across an issue that seems to undermine much of what we've been discussing. Fathers, the record shows, do not seem to contribute much to children's *survival*. The ultimate purpose of good fathering (as well as mothering) is to ensure the survival of children. If the presence of fathers doesn't boost children's chances of surviving to have children themselves, does anything else matter?

The study that posed this question was published in 2008 by two British researchers. They analyzed forty-five studies looking at the effect of family members on children's survival rates. The idea was to determine whether the presence of a father improves children's survival, or whether other family members might be more important. The study, by Rebecca Sear of the London School of Economics and Ruth Mace of the anthropology department at University College London, is titled "Who Keeps Children Alive?" Unlike most scientific papers, it begins with a provocative observation: "Children pose a problem." Human families have children about three years apart—a short interval compared to close relatives such as the orangutan, where the interval between births is about eight years, and chimpanzees, where it is four to five years. That means that human families are especially burdened with the need to raise two or more children simultaneously. Human mothers need help. But it's unclear where that help is coming from.

The traditional answer has been that the help comes from fathers, as parents cooperate to raise their children. But Sear and Mace are interested in another possibility: grandmothers. Too old to have more children of their own, they are free to help with their grandchildren. It's possible that menopause and the high human birthrate evolved hand in hand. The ability to have more children evolved along with the opportunity to get help from grandmothers, and the fruits of this evolutionary path are with us today. Some researchers have found that children with older female relatives are better nourished, and there's evidence that gathering food—usually a woman's task—contributes more nourishment to children than does hunting—the men's job. (There are exceptions to these findings. In the Arctic, hunters, such as the Inuit, derive almost all their calories from the hunt. There isn't much to gather under the snow and ice, and children couldn't survive on a hunt in the harsh weather.)

The analysis by Sear and Mace supports these ideas. They found, first of all, that the worst thing that can happen to a child is the death of its mother, which is clearly associated with higher mortality. But in some studies, this applied only to very young children. After age two, children who were suddenly motherless no longer faced such dismal odds of survival. "Clearly, two-year-old children are not self-sufficient, so the good survival prospects of children who lose their mothers in later childhood must be due to other individuals taking over child care and provisioning," they write. But fathers "frequently make no difference to child survival." Of the fifteen studies that included an appropriate mathematical analysis of the statistics, "there is no association between the death of a father and the death of a child." To put it another way, a child who loses its father faces no increased risk of dying. Can that possibly be true?

Sear and Mace are cautious in their interpretation of these results. They suggest that the importance of fathers in providing food has been overestimated; the children are getting it from somewhere. "Fathers may play more important roles in the lives of older children, teaching them subsistence skills and enhancing their marriage and fertility prospects," they write. But it might be easier to compensate for lost fathers' contributions than for those of mothers. That is where grandmothers come in. "Maternal grandmothers tend to improve child survival, as do elder sibling helpers at the nest. Paternal grandmothers are frequently beneficial, but show rather more variation than maternal grandmothers in their effects on child survival." They emphasize that these links are not causal relationships; they are associations. And this overview deals solely with the role of fathers in preventing children's deaths, and so it doesn't conflict with much of the research by others showing that fathers make important contributions to such predictors of success in life as their children's cognitive skills, social skills, and competence in school. What the study does do is provide a richer picture of the contributions of relatives and of the differences between mothers and fathers.

The study also has important implications for politicians and policy makers who believe the nuclear family is the best setting in which to raise children. That widely held belief has been endorsed by many politicians and public figures; it's an article of faith among millions of Americans. And it's certainly true, as we've seen, that we should encourage fathers' involvement with their children—the research supports that in many different ways. But this is not the exclusive model for families. Other arrangements can work well, too. If the absence of fathers doesn't increase the rate of childhood mortality, it could be because when fathers are absent, other relatives can step in to compensate for that absence. Policy makers who want to encourage fathers' involvement with their children are right to do so, but they might want to take a flexible approach. As we've said before, fathers are not *essential* for the healthy development of children. But as the many examples I've presented show, fathers can give children many, many important advantages.

And despite the findings of Sear and Mace, the positives outweigh the negatives with regard to fathers' contributions to their kids. Fathers should spend as much time as they can with their toddlers and school-age children. And they shouldn't feel compelled to prop flash cards in front of them or read sixth-grade books to third-graders. They should spend more time playing.

SEVEN

Teenagers: Absence, Puberty, and Faithful Voles

In 2013, the psychologists Sarah E. Hill and Danielle J. DelPriore departed from the usual formality of scientific papers and began their report with an anecdote from the news. The story they told came from Frayser High School in Memphis, Tennessee. Frayser had made national news in 2011 when officials came to a disturbing realization: about one in five of its female students was either pregnant or had recently given birth. Memphis officials disputed the exact figures, but they admitted that Frayser had a problem. One local official blamed the disturbing rate of teen pregnancy on television. She pointed to the MTV shows *16 and Pregnant* and *Teen Mom*. "So much of our society is sexually oriented," she said, arguing that the fixation on sex was enticing the girls to have unprotected sex earlier and more often. A lot of us might say the same thing. We know that teenagers are impressionable, and the idea that they would be swayed by MTV makes sense. They adopt fashions and products they see on television; why not sexual behavior?

But Hill and DelPriore, who are at Texas Christian University, took note of a more subtle fact about Tennessee: nearly one in four households was headed by a single mother.

For Hill and DelPriore, that was a tipoff that something entirely different was going on. "Researchers have revealed a robust association between father absence—both physical and psychological—and accelerated reproductive development and sexual risk-taking in daughters," they wrote. You might expect sexual maturation to be deeply inscribed in teenagers' genes, and not likely affected by something as arbitrary and unpredictable as whether or not they live in the same house as their fathers. But the association is quite clear. The problem comes in trying to explain it. How could a change in a girl's environment—the departure of her father—influence something as central to biology as her reproductive development?

I put that question to Hill. "When dad is absent," she explained, "it basically provides young girls with a cue about what the future holds in terms of the mating system they are born into." When a girl's family is disrupted, and her father leaves or isn't close to her, she gets the message that men don't stay for long, and her partner might not stick around, either. So finding a man requires quick action. The sooner she's ready to have children, the better. She can't consciously decide to enter puberty earlier, but her biology takes over, subconsciously. She enters puberty earlier, gets pregnant sooner, and has more children quickly. "This would help facilitate what we call, in evolutionary sciences, a faster reproductive strategy," Hill said.

In contrast, a girl who grows up in a family in which the bond between her parents is more secure, and who has a father who lives in the home, might well (subconsciously) adopt a slower reproductive strategy. She might conclude that she can take a bit more time to start having children. She can be more thorough in her preparation. In this scenario, men stick around; there's time. "If you're going to have two invested parents, you're investing more reproductive resources. If the expectation is you are not going to receive these investments, you should shift toward the faster strategy," Hill explained.

These links between fathers and the age at which girls enter puberty are associations. We see, by looking at populations of teenage girls, that an absent father and early puberty go together. But the ideas about *why* this happens are speculation. There's no proof—at least, not yet—that the behavior of fathers *causes* these changes in their daughters. Ideally, the experiment that would answer this question would be to assemble a group of families as research subjects and randomly assign some of the fathers to abandon their families and others to stay. Obviously, this is not a proposal likely to win approval from ethics boards. So what is the next best thing? Hill and DelPriore designed an experiment in which young women—some of them teenagers and others just past their teen years—were reminded of an incident in which their father supported them, and then were encouraged to think about a time he was *not* there for them. The idea was to see whether the different memories would change the girls' attitudes toward sexual behavior. The way Hill and DelPriore prodded their subjects to bring those memories to the fore was to ask them to write about those experiences. After they finished writing, they would be asked about their attitudes toward sexual behavior. If the hypothesis was correct, memories of unpleasant father experiences would lead the young women to express more favorable views of risky sexual behavior. Pleasant memories of their fathers should push them in the opposite direction.

And that's what happened. Young women became "more

sexually unrestricted" after recalling an incident in which their father was disengaged, Hill explained. "They reported having more favorable attitudes toward short-term sexual encounters; they didn't see love as necessary for sex to occur." Further experiments showed that father disengagement didn't change women's views of other kinds of risky behavior; they weren't more likely to ride a bike without a helmet. The effect was limited to sex.

Hill told me that her research rests heavily on work by Bruce J. Ellis of the University of Arizona, who helped establish the connection between father absence and adverse outcomes for daughters. Ellis calls himself an evolutionary developmental psychologist. He's interested in whether Darwin's theory of natural selection can help explain how children's environments shape their development—precisely the question that came up in Hill's study. His work on fathers began in the late 1990s, with efforts to test an interesting theory proposed by other evolution-oriented psychologists. The idea was that early experiences could affect children's reproductive strategies. Early paternal involvement seems to "set" the reproductive strategy that girls use later in their lives.

Ellis quickly discovered that there was something about fathers that gave them a unique role in regulating their daughters' development—especially their sexual development—around the time of puberty. In a series of studies beginning in 1999, he found that when girls had a warm relationship with their fathers and spent a lot of time with them in the first five to seven years of their lives, they had a reduced risk of early puberty, early initiation of sex, and teen pregnancy.

Ellis continued this work until the early 2000s, demonstrating the phenomenon in different ways, but he became increasingly frustrated. Clearly, the *association* between fathers' presence or absence and daughters' maturation was profound. But he could not determine whether paternal behavior caused the consequences he was seeing in the daughters. The idea that father absence was responsible for early puberty in daughters was compelling, but it wasn't the only possible explanation. An alternative was that girls who begin puberty early and engage in risky sexual behavior do so because of genes they've inherited from their parents—the same genes, perhaps, that led to the truncated parental relationship. Fathers whose genes might be linked to their infidelity might pass those genes on to their daughters, where they could be associated with risky sexual behavior and early puberty. A third guess was that something else in the family's environment was responsible for the accelerated development of the daughters, not their fathers.

Ellis came up with an innovative way to address the question. He considered families in which divorced parents had two daughters separated by an average of seven years in age. When the parents divorced, the older sister would have had seven more years with her father than the younger sister. To put it another way, the younger sister would be "exposed" to seven more years of father absence than her older sibling. If father absence causes early puberty and risky behavior, then the younger daughter should show more of that behavior than her older sibling. And genes or the family's environment would not confuse the results because the genes are randomly distributed among the daughters. It was something close to a naturally occurring experiment, Ellis realized. He called it a "quasi-experiment."

Ellis recruited families with two daughters. Some were

families in which the parents divorced; others were intact families, to be used as a control group. He wanted to answer two questions: Was the age at which the girls had their first menstrual period affected by the length of time they spent with a father in the house? And did that age vary depending upon how their fathers behaved? The second question was added because fathers with a history of violence, depression, drug abuse, or imprisonment can affect children's development, and the researchers wanted to know whether those things might also affect the timing of puberty.

Ellis's suspicions were confirmed. Younger sisters in divorced families, who spent more time without a father in the house, had their first periods an average of eleven months earlier than their older sisters—but only in homes in which the men had behaved badly as fathers. Ellis told me that while they expected to find that the behavior of the fathers affected their daughters, "we were surprised to get as big an effect as we did." The conclusion was that growing up with an emotionally or physically distant father in early to middle childhood could be "a key life transition" that alters sexual development.

The next step Ellis took was to look at whether these circumstances could affect the involvement of girls in risky sexual behavior. The correlation between the behavior of fathers and risky behavior by their daughters had already been established. An increased risk of pregnancy or of infection with a sexually transmitted disease was clearly more common in daughters of disrupted families or daughters whose relationships with their fathers were marked by harsh conflict, little warmth or support, and lack of parental supervision. Once again, however, Ellis was interested in sorting out whether these were associated because of external or genetic factors, or whether the emotional distance of the fathers had caused the daughters' risky sexual behavior.

He again sought sisters from divorced families. This time he turned to Craigslist and posted announcements in several cities that began, "SISTERS WANTED!" The criteria were very specific: He was looking for families with two sisters at least four years apart in age and currently between the ages of eighteen and thirty-six. He limited his search to families in which the birth parents separated or divorced when the younger sister was under fourteen years of age. Ellis and his colleagues were able to recruit 101 pairs of sisters, some from families in which the parents had divorced, and, using a different ad, some whose parents had not.

This time, the researchers found that risky sexual behavior in daughters wasn't simply related to how long they'd lived with their fathers but to the combination of how long they lived with their fathers and what the fathers did in the time they spent with their daughters. "Girls that grew up with a high-quality father—and who lived with him for longer periods of time—showed the lowest level of risky sexual behavior," Ellis said. "Their younger sisters, who spent less time living with him, tended to show the highest level of risky sexual behavior." In other words, more years of living with a father who was involved with his children protected girls from risky sexual behavior.

The next question, then, was this: Exactly how do fathers exert this effect on their daughters? One possible explanation, as unlikely as it might seem, is that a father's scent affects his daughters' behavior. Many animals emit pheromones, chemical messengers that can be picked up by others and can alter their behavior. "There is certainly evidence from animal research, in a number of species, that exposure to the pheromones of unrelated males can accelerate pubertal development, and some evidence that exposure to pheromones of a father can slow it down," Ellis explained. "If you take a prepubescent female mouse, a mouse that has not gone through sexual maturation yet, and you stick her in a cage where an adult male has been living and the litter in that cage is saturated with his pheromones—that will cause her to go through puberty more quickly. Just living in that cage."

Similar effects have been seen with other animals. If the same is true of humans, pheromones could help to explain how the presence or absence of fathers affects their daughters—although that remains an untested hypothesis. The evidence for the action of pheromones in humans is fuzzier, but some research suggests that women who sleep with a male partner have more regular menstrual cycles, perhaps because of the presence of the male's pheromones.

As we finished our conversation, Ellis brought up something I had been wondering about. What effect does father presence or absence have on sons? He told me that we don't yet know about sons, and that he himself hasn't studied them yet. His hypothesis is that a father's involvement could have a different effect on sons, enhancing a competitive urge and spurring sons to achieve more when they grow up and leave the family. His speculation echoes what we learned about imprinted genes in mice: that a male-imprinted gene does different things in daughters and in sons. In females, it affects the way they care for their young, and in males, the way they compete for mates. A son's inability to succeed in life could be the human counterpart of a male mouse's deficiencies as a suitor.

•

One of the ways we know fathers have close and conse-
quential relationships with their children is that men change
when they become fathers—and the changes stay with
them. We've seen briefly how blood levels of hormones such
as oxytocin and prolactin change in animals in response to
fatherhood, and that those changes can profoundly affect
the behavior of fathers and their relationships with their
offspring. Now we can look at those changes more closely,
and see how they relate to similar changes in us.

One of the best animals for exploring the role of hormones in fathers is the vole. Like mice and rats, voles are
close to us in evolutionary terms. As always, we should be
careful about assuming that what's true in voles is true in
men. But as we've seen, experiments with animals often
give us our first glimpse of what we later find out to be true
in humans. So voles are worth paying attention to.

Voles, like deer mice, come in a couple of varieties—
the prairie vole and the montane vole. The prairie vole is
monogamous, and when it mates, the male guards the female. Oxytocin governs much of this behavior. Give a female
oxytocin, and she will bond with whatever male is near:
Love the one you're with. If her oxytocin receptors are
blocked, she won't bond to a male, even after mating. But
this doesn't work in montane voles, a closely related promiscuous species. Pump them up with oxytocin and they're
still promiscuous.

Thomas R. Insel, a psychiatrist and the director of the
National Institute of Mental Health, studied voles for
fifteen years when he ran the Yerkes Regional Primate
Research Center in Atlanta. The two species of voles are

99 percent identical, Insel has said, but it's the remaining 1 percent that makes them interesting—because it leads to very different social behavior.

Prairie voles are social creatures. Males and females form long-lasting monogamous bonds, and both parents share the care of their young. Both male and female montane voles abandon their young shortly after birth and do not form long-lasting bonds with one another. In the laboratory, Insel observed that prairie voles spent more than 50 percent of their time huddling with their mates. When a prairie vole dies, its mate will usually live alone rather than choose a new partner. Insel and his colleagues wanted to know what it was in the scant bit of DNA that differed between these two species that made them so different with regard to mating and parenting. The answer, he believed, could shed light on the mating characteristics of humans as well.

It soon emerged that one of the key factors underlying vole behavior was indeed oxytocin, which also functions as a neurotransmitter—that is, it is involved in signaling within the brain. Oxytocin is associated with social behavior, childbirth, nursing, sex, and maternal bonding. It causes the uterus to contract during labor, and a synthetic form of it, Pitocin, is routinely used to stimulate or induce labor in pregnant women.

In 1992, Insel looked in the brains of prairie and montane voles for oxytocin receptors—the molecular entryways where oxytocin can attach and allow neurons to respond. He found oxytocin receptors in half a dozen places in the brains of monogamous prairie voles—including some in an area called the nucleus accumbens, the brain's reward center, which is where cocaine exerts its pleasurable effects. In the polygamous montane voles, in contrast, he found little evidence of oxytocin receptors in those places. To check the findings, he looked at the brains of two other kinds of voles—one monogamous, and one not—and found similar discrepancies. When he looked for such differences related to other hormones, he couldn't find them. And there was one other intriguing finding. When montane vole females gave birth, the distribution of the oxytocin receptors shifted in certain regions in their brains just as the mothers began to demonstrate maternal behavior.

Males also produce oxytocin, but for them another chemical very similar to oxytocin—known as vasopressin—seems to be the key substance responsible for bonding. In voles, it helps create the bond between males and females. As is the case with oxytocin, the monogamous males have vasopressin receptors in many places where the polygamous voles do not. In 2004, Larry J. Young of Emory University—a collaborator of Insel's in some of those early experiments—conducted an experiment related to vasopressin that he describes as "mind-blowing." He and his colleagues took the gene for the vasopressin receptor from a monogamous vole and injected it into the brain of a nonmonogamous vole known as a meadow vole. They injected it into the part of the brain that's related to reward and addiction. "When we put these transformed meadow voles with a female and allowed them to mate and then we tested them, these animals had formed a bond with that partner." In every other regard, they behaved exactly as before. "This shows that you can transform behavior, even complex social behavior like bonding, just by changing the expression of a single gene in a single brain area."

The researchers were also interested in whether the boost in vasopressin receptors would alter the meadow voles' normally indifferent paternal behavior. They didn't find differences in such behaviors as how much time males spent licking or huddling with their offspring. But the fathers approached their offspring more quickly and spent more time with the pups than males that didn't get the boost in vasopressin receptors. Various experiments showed that some manipulations of the hormone would block bonding but not fathering behavior, or vice versa. The conclusion was that bonding and fathering are both related to vasopressin, but that each involves a distinct circuit in the brain—and that those circuits differ from one species of vole to another.

C. Sue Carter, a neuroscientist at the University of Illinois at Chicago and the codirector of the university's Brain-Body Center, did the original research on male prairie voles—specifically, on what happens when a male vole meets his baby. Among the social, bonding, monogamous prairie voles, males are more likely to engage in spontaneous parenting behavior than virgin females. "A female vole who hasn't had babies is not parental when exposed to a baby," she told me. Among males, on the other hand, about 80 percent spontaneously respond to babies as if they already know how to be fathers. "It's so mysterious," she says. "There's no hormonal priming, they haven't been pregnant, they haven't seen a baby since they were babies themselves." Females begin to behave as parents once they've given birth. The idea is that exposure to the babies probably leads to hormonal changes. But, Carter said, when the male hasn't been exposed, he's still parental. "Why do they become instantly parental, and why does the female not? The baby is like some magic potion, and for some reason males are more sensitive than females."

Carter and a colleague, William M. Kenkel, looked at hormonal changes in voles to see whether they could account for this mysterious phenomenon. They found that when males who'd never seen infants were exposed to one, their blood oxytocin levels increased within ten minutes. When these males were later handled by experimenters, they didn't show the rise in stress hormones that usually occurs when they are picked up. While this is only a first step in understanding the changes that occur in voles, it shows that oxytocin is involved, as it is in the formation of pair bonds—meaning that mating and parental behavior are related. On top of this, Carter and Kenkel also found that when a father is in the presence of a baby, its heart rate jumps up. "These animals are in a high state of vigilance," Carter says. "We suspect that a cocktail of oxytocin and vasopressin works together in male voles to permit both nurturance and defense of the offspring."

What we're really concerned about, however, is this: Does vole fathering have an effect on the pups? And if so, what can this tell us about human fathers? Hugh Broders of Saint Mary's University in Halifax, Nova Scotia, and his colleagues raised a group of voles in normal circumstances—with both parents participating in their care. And they raised another group in which fathers were removed and the pups were raised only by their mother. The mothers' behavior didn't change, but the effects on the pups were striking. The pups raised without a father displayed higher levels of anxiety, reduced activity in the cage, and lower levels of social behavior. Something important in their emotional and social makeup wasn't right.

•

Some research now being done on human fathers is complementing what's being learned from other animals. In a paper in 2008, Hasse Walum of the Karolinska Institute in Sweden and his colleagues looked at a particular vasopressin receptor gene, responsible for one of the molecules that vasopressin connects with in order to exert its effects. This receptor is known to have an important influence on mating in voles. A form of this gene exists in humans, but researchers didn't know whether it also had an effect on human pair bonding. The researchers analyzed genetic data on their subjects, and also assessed the quality of their marriages using a standard questionnaire. They found that men who carry one particular form of this receptor gene—known as the "RS3 genotype"—are less likely to get married and more likely to have marital problems if they do. The gene even affects their wives, who tend to have a lower opinion of the quality of their marriage than women married to men with other forms of the receptor gene. They concluded that the human situation is related to that in voles: vasopressin helps to shape marital relationships.

In 2012, Walum and colleagues took the research a step further. This time, they looked at whether variations in an oxytocin receptor gene in women would have a similar effect on marital behavior. And it did: women carrying a particular version of the receptor gene had more marital problems, and their spouses also reported that they had poorer relationships. Interestingly, the gene variant was also associated with social problems in the women's childhoods—problems similar to those seen in autism. Women who experienced social difficulties as children, such as trouble bonding with friends, were less able to form good marital bonds as adults. This, too, the researchers reported, parallels what has been found in voles.

This is precisely how research is supposed to work, and why research with animals is important. It allows scientists to make suppositions about the role of oxytocin and vasopressin in humans, and to develop hypotheses. In recent years, researchers have done many experiments involving humans and oxytocin, often simply giving people a sniff of oxytocin in various circumstances and watching to see what happens. They've found that it can reduce stress, encourage trust, make it easier to ignore angry faces, increase recognition of fear in faces, increase motivation, increase "envy and gloating over monetary gain or loss" of another participant, and even, in patients with autism spectrum disorder, boost social interaction with characters in a computer game.

Oxytocin's importance in father-child relationships—and whether administering it as a drug could change them—was the subject of a study by Dutch researchers. They enlisted seventeen fathers and their toddlers, and observed them in two separate play sessions of fifteen minutes each, within a week. The mean age of the fathers was thirty-eight, and their children ranged in age from a year and a half to five. In one session, each father was given a whiff of oxytocin; in the other, he was given a placebo. The hypothesis was that oxytocin would increase the responsiveness of fathers to their children—making the fathers more encouraging and stimulating—because oxytocin should enhance their sensitivity to the cues of their infants.

The hypothesis proved to be correct. Oxytocin-juiced fathers "stimulated their child's exploration and autonomy in a more optimal way" than the same fathers when given a placebo. They also showed fewer negative responses, such as impatience, discontent, and rolling their eyes. The speculation is that oxytocin activates the release of dopamine, a neurotransmitter associated with rewards, and thus reinforces desirable behavior in the fathers. The researcher claimed that this was the first experimental evidence that oxytocin could increase responsiveness in fathers.

The Dutch study meshed nicely with one done by Ruth Feldman and her colleagues at Bar-Ilan University in Israel. Feldman, you'll recall, was the person interested in synchrony—the idea that parents match and encourage infants' positive emotions when they are face-to-face. Feldman and her team looked at what happens to oxytocin in parents after they've had pleasant interactions with their children. They watched, took notes, and videotaped 112 mothers and fathers playing with their four- to six-month-old infants. The researchers took blood and saliva samples from the parents to measure oxytocin levels before the session, and took a saliva sample again fifteen minutes after the session.

Mothers and fathers had different reactions. Mothers who "provided high levels of affectionate contact" showed an increase in oxytocin after interacting with their infants. A similar rise was not seen in mothers expressing low levels of affection. For fathers, oxytocin rose not with affectionate contact, but with stimulation of the infants and play that involved exploration. Oxytocin, in other words, increased in men in response to typical father-child interaction: rough-and-tumble play. Biparental care is "not biologically necessary," they wrote, but contact between fathers and infants was clearly linked to the biology of fathers, as indicated by the rise in oxytocin following play. They concluded that the findings "have important implications for social policy and emphasize the need to provide opportunities for daily contact between fathers and infants during the first months of fatherhood in order to trigger the biological basis of fathering."

After observing the rise in oxytocin in fathers, Feldman and her colleagues decided to administer a dose of oxytocin to fathers to see how that would affect both the fathers and their infants, who would not be given oxytocin. They recruited thirty-five fathers with five-month-old infants, gave the fathers a dose of oxytocin or a placebo, and then assessed the results. The oxytocin dose boosted fathers' engagement and bonding during play sessions. And while the infants were not given oxytocin, giving the drug to their fathers raised the infants' oxytocin levels, their responsiveness, and their engagement with their fathers. The results showed that oxytocin administration to one partner can have effects on the other. The discovery underscores the importance of oxytocin in the transmission of social behavior from parents to children.

Besides revealing a vital biological connection between fathers and their children, the study also suggested a novel way of treating children with social disorders: treat their parents with oxytocin. Children who are born prematurely, or whose parents are depressed, for example, can miss some of the important early bonding experiences that lead to the development of appropriate social behavior. And the study had implications for children with autism. Giving oxytocin to the parents of those children might deepen the parent-child relationships that autism can disrupt. That change, in turn, could boost levels of oxytocin in the children—and their ability to interact socially with others.

Feldman and her group also discovered that the hormone prolactin has an important role to play for fathers and their children. As we saw earlier, prolactin, which is related to lactation in women, rises in fathers near the end of their partner's pregnancy and after birth. In men, prolactin is related to the way fathers play and their encouragement of children's desire to explore, itself a characteristic of father play. The researchers speculated that as fathers become more familiar with their infants over time, the prolactin and oxytocin systems create new connections between them. Both the emotional connection and the exploratory encouragement are key aspects of attachment between fathers and their children.

Feldman reflected on the importance of the work on oxytocin and relationships: "Our responsibility as caregivers, scientists, policy makers, mental health professionals, and concerned citizens is that every young child should be given the opportunity to learn how to love, and every young parent should receive the guidance to make it happen." Compared to the language used in most scientific papers, that's lyric poetry.

It's not surprising that parents are important in shaping their children's behavior. But what about the flip side of that? Can children, including teenagers, shape their parents' behavior? Researchers have turned up a variety of interesting answers to that question. One study of fathers and teenage children's behavior asked not only how parenting influences risky sexual behavior but also how such behavior in turn influences parenting. In particular, how do fathers react when they find out their children are at risk?

Teenagers who engage regularly in activities with their families (such as eating meals together, participating in religious activities, or simply having fun with one another) were less likely to engage in risky sexual behaviors—sexual intercourse at an early age, frequent intercourse, having multiple partners, and being careless about birth control. The same was true for children whose fathers were more knowledgeable about their children's friends and activities. This confirmed earlier research. The surprising new finding was this: some theories of the family predict that parents will react to their kids' risky behavior by becoming less engaged and showing more hostility. But in this case, risky behavior led fathers to become more involved and more knowledgeable about their children's activities. Mothers showed no significant reaction.

Another study on fathers and adolescents is one we can file in the category of "unfortunate things fathers contribute to their children." Heather Sipsma and colleagues at the Yale School of Public Health were interested in the children of men who become fathers as teenagers. Teen parents usually have more limited education and financial resources than older parents, and teen parenthood can disrupt the normal psychological development of children. The children of teen parents are also at higher risk of abuse and neglect than children of older parents. Daughters of teen mothers are more likely than other girls to become teen mothers themselves. But Sipsma and her colleagues could find no information on whether the sons of teenage fathers were at increased risk of repeating their fathers' history.

It's important to know whether that's the case because of the adverse consequences of teen fatherhood. It's been associated with low socioeconomic status, reduced educational accomplishments, and delinquency. Sipsma and her colleagues found that the sons of teenage fathers were 1.8 times more likely to become adolescent fathers than were the sons of older fathers. They called it "an intergenerational cycle of risk" for young fatherhood—that is, teen fathers tended to pass it on to the next generation. The broader conclusion was that programs aimed at reducing teenage pregnancy should focus on fathers as well as mothers. Indeed, as Sipsma noted, men are an important but neglected group in reproductive health.

The way fathers treat their adolescents can have long-lasting consequences, stretching into adulthood. As parents of teenagers know, it's often hard to know how to respond to the crises, struggles, school challenges, and social difficulties that are a normal part of the passage from childhood to adulthood. What we do *matters*—but it's so often hard to know what we should do. One key feature of good parenting, however, is to create a situation in which teenagers feel they are accepted by their parents rather than rejected. That's often easier to say than to do—especially when, say, they show up with a tattoo or call you from the principal's office.

Ronald P. Rohner at the University of Connecticut has spent some years looking at the consequences for children who perceive themselves to be accepted by their parents, and comparing their outcomes with what happens to children and teenagers who feel they were rejected by their parents. He thinks that parental acceptance influences important aspects of personality. Children who are accepted by their parents are independent and emotionally stable; they are more apt to have strong self-esteem and a positive worldview. Those who feel they were rejected show the opposite—hostility, feelings of inadequacy, instability, and a negative worldview. Rohner analyzed data from thirty-six studies on parental acceptance and rejection and found that they supported his theory. Both maternal and paternal acceptance were associated with these positive personality characteristics: father's love and acceptance are, in this regard, at least as important as that of mother. The influence of father's rejection can be greater than that of mothers. That's not necessarily good news for fathers—it increases the pressure on them to get it right. "The great emphasis on mothers and mothering in America has led to an inappropriate tendency to blame mothers for children's behavior problems and maladjustment when, in fact, fathers are often more implicated than mothers in the development of problems such as these," Rohner explained.

Empathy is another important characteristic that we hope our teenagers will develop, and fathers seem to have a surprisingly important role here, too. Richard Koestner, a psychologist at McGill University in Montreal, looked back at seventy-five men and women who had been part of a study at Yale University in the 1950s, when they were children. When Koestner and his colleagues looked at all the factors in the children's lives that might have affected how empathetic they became as adults, one factor dwarfed all the others: how much time their fathers spent with them. "We were amazed to find that how affectionate parents were with their children made no difference in empathy," Koestner said. "And we were astounded at how strong the father's influence was."

Melanie Mallers, a psychologist at California State University, Fullerton, also found that sons who have fond childhood memories of their fathers were more likely to be able to handle the day-to-day stresses of adulthood. Around the same time, a team from the University of Toronto put adults in an fMRI scanner to assess their reaction to the faces of their parents, and how that might differ from their reaction to the faces of strangers. The brains of the subjects responded differently to mothers and to fathers. Mothers' faces elicited more activity in parts of the brain associated with face processing, among others. But the faces of fathers elicited activity in the caudate, a deep brain structure associated with feelings of love.

The importance of fathers in ensuring the health of their offspring extends beyond their own children. As we've seen, imprinted genes, which carry a chemical stamp marking which parent they came from, have consequences not only for children but also for grandchildren. These are the genes that engage in a tug-of-war at conception and must be kept in balance to assure children's health. Imprinted genes that children receive from their mothers and fathers affect what kind of parents they themselves will be when the time comes—a finding that raises the stakes on everything fathers do for their children.

EIGHT

Older Fathers: The Rewards and Risks of Waiting

Stroll through parks and playgrounds in many parts of the country these days, and you're likely to see a lot of older men pushing strollers. You know who they are—you hesitate before starting a conversation, because you don't know whether you will be talking to dad or grandpa.

This confusion was wonderfully captured by the writer and director Nora Ephron in *You've Got Mail*. Joe Fox, played by Tom Hanks, and a boy and girl walk into the bookshop owned by Kathleen, played by Meg Ryan. The girl, Annabel, refers to Tom Hanks as "my nephew," and Kathleen says, "Oh, I don't really think that's your nephew." But it's true. And the boy, Matt, tells her that Joe is his brother. Joe says that's right. "Annabel is my grandfather's daughter. And Matt is my father's son. We are an American family."

The Foxes might not be a typical American family, but it's not that unusual for older men to become fathers, as I found out when I became an older father myself. My wife, Elizabeth, was forty when our first son was born. We knew about the things than can go wrong in the children of older mothers. First, we worried about whether she'd be able to get pregnant. Then, when she did, we worried that she might have a miscarriage. And we worried about Down syndrome, more common in the children of older mothers. Elizabeth had all the tests to rule out Down syndrome and some other possible genetic abnormalities. The tests were normal. That wasn't a guarantee that the baby would be okay, but it was reassuring nonetheless.

The day after our son was born, while we were still bleary-eyed from the late-night delivery, we were aimlessly flipping channels on a television bolted to the wall of Elizabeth's hospital room when we caught part of a news report about an increased risk of autism in the children of older fathers. Until then, all we'd thought about, and worried about, was Elizabeth's age. Now I was hearing that *my* age could pose a risk to our baby, too. I was fifty-five. The report we were seeing on the television applied to us. We had never heard anything like this before. I mumbled something about the unfortunate timing of that report, when it was too late for us to do anything about it, and we flipped to another channel. We didn't talk about it; I hoped Elizabeth would fall asleep and forget it. I hoped I would, too.

But I couldn't forget it. When we got home a couple of days later, I looked up the report. Researchers were explaining that the children of fathers forty and over had a six-fold increase in the risk of autism compared to kids whose fathers were under thirty. I found the study on the Web. It said children of fathers over fifty had a tenfold greater risk of autism. And there was more bad news. "Advanced paternal age," as researchers called it, has also been linked to an increased risk of early-onset bipolar disorder, birth defects, cleft lip and palate, water on the brain, dwarfism, miscarriage, premature birth, and "decreased intellectual capacity."

What was most frightening to me, as someone with mental illness in the family, was that older fatherhood was also associated with an increased risk of schizophrenia. The risk rises with each passing year. The child of a forty-year-old father had a 2 percent chance of having schizophrenia—double the risk of children whose fathers are under thirty. A forty-year-old man's risk of having a child with schizophrenia was the same as a forty-year-old woman's risk of having a child with Down syndrome.

Because I was over fifty, the risk that our son would develop schizophrenia was even higher—3 percent. The illness usually appears in the late teens or early twenties, and there's no way to know who will develop it until then. It will be two decades before we know whether either of our two young boys is affected. Assuming we both survive, I'll be in my seventies, and Elizabeth in her sixties. That's a long time to wait before exhaling. (More recent research, as we'll see, has told us even more.)

The study seemed to me to raise a disturbing question: Why didn't we know this? The female biological clock is talked about so often that it's become a sitcom cliché. Why do we hear so little about these biological clocks in men? Here was evidence of a very important contribution that fathers make to their children—a potentially harmful one.

I wondered how many American children had older fathers, and whether the number of older fathers was increasing, as it seems to be. I called the U.S. Census Bureau. The bureau, it turns out, does not count older fathers. This seemed a surprising admission by an agency that counts all fathers (70.1 million), the number married with children under eighteen (24.4 million), single fathers (1.96 million), and even the number of sporting goods stores where you

can buy dad a fishing rod for Father's Day (21,418). As for
the number of older fathers, Robert Bernstein, a public
affairs specialist at the bureau, told me, "We tried to collect
this information many years ago, and the reporting on men
was not so reliable, so we stopped asking." The reason this
was too tough to do, according to an anonymous e-mail I
received later from the Census Bureau, was that "a lot of
women get pregnant and don't know who the fathers are—or
the fathers don't care."

Information is available from birth certificates, however, and it's collected by the National Center for Health
Statistics, part of the Centers for Disease Control and Prevention. That data shows that the number of births to men
forty to forty-nine nearly tripled between 1980 and 2004, rising from 120,702 to 328,465. (The numbers have risen only
slightly since then.) Much of the jump was due to an increase
in the overall population. But there has been a shift, over
the past generation, toward more men becoming fathers
when they are older—a trend beyond what can be accounted
for by the growth in population. Birthrates for men in their
forties (a number that takes population growth into account) have risen by up to 40 percent since 1980—while
birthrates for men under thirty were falling by as much as
21 percent.

This represents a sharp change from earlier decades.
The number of older fathers in the 1940s and 1950s was
even higher than it is now, but for a different reason: most
men started out as young fathers, but families were larger,
and many dads slipped past forty before they had their last
child. The number of older fathers fell through the 1960s,
and began to climb again after reaching a low in 1975, when
women began entering the workforce in larger numbers.

While this was happening, men and women were increasingly delaying marriage. In 2011, according to the Census Bureau, the median age at first marriage for men was almost twenty-nine, up from twenty-five in 1980. The Census Bureau doesn't collect data on the age at which fathers have their first child, but Matthew Weinshenker, a sociologist at Fordham University in New York, used a variety of surveys to estimate that the percentage of fathers who are having their first child after age thirty-five rose from 2 percent in the 1970s to nearly 17 percent in the 1990s. "The percentage of first-time fathers who are older has exploded over the past few decades," he said.

Changes in the workplace have made childbearing decisions more difficult for many couples. As we've seen, many employees are now subject to far more demands from their employers than in the past. Changes like these make it harder for people to carve out time for their children. And most feel they can't refuse to do what their employers ask. "Among more highly educated people, I think you see them trying to get their careers established so they can have more flexibility when they have children," said Ellen Galinsky of the Families and Work Institute. "I hear all the time that people want to feel that their employer knows they're valuable, so they'll have the flexibility they want when they have kids—taking leave, taking time off."

The medical risks associated with being an older father might be partly offset by the commitments that many older parents make to their children. Brian Powell, a sociologist at Indiana University, studies the social, cultural and economic resources that parents devote to their children. When he began his research, he expected to find a mixed picture in older parents. "We assumed there would be trade-offs, that older parents might have more economic resources, but the trade-off would be less personal involvement, less involvement with the schools—less energy." Their research proved that assumption to be wrong. Older parents were deeply involved in school, ballet classes, piano lessons, their children's friends—and they devoted more economic resources to all these things. "It turns out, the older the parent, the better it is for the child," Powell said.

Another reason for the increased number of older fathers is the high prevalence of divorce and remarriage, said Linda J. Waite, a sociologist at the University of Chicago. While men in first marriages are typically one and a half to two years older than their wives, men in second marriages are, on average, fifteen years older than their wives. "About half of marriages end in divorce, so remarriage for men is pretty common. They tend to marry someone younger, and often that person hasn't had kids and wants to have kids," she said.

The idea that a father's age could affect the health of his children was first hinted at a century ago by an unusually perceptive and industrious doctor in private practice in Stuttgart, Germany. Wilhelm Weinberg was a loner who devoted much of his time to caring for the poor, including delivering some 3,500 babies during a forty-year career. He also managed to publish 160 scientific papers, without the benefit of colleagues, students, or grants. His papers, written in German, didn't attract much attention initially; most geneticists spoke English. It wasn't until years later that some of Weinberg's papers were recognized as landmarks.

One was a 1912 study noting that a form of dwarfism called achondroplasia was more common among the last-born children in families than among the firstborn. Weinberg didn't know why that was so, but he speculated that it might be related to the age of the parents, who were of course older when their later children were born. Weinberg's prescient observation was confirmed decades later when research showed that he was half right: the risk of dwarfism rose with the father's age but not the mother's.

Since then, about twenty ailments have been linked to paternal age, including progeria, the disorder of rapid aging; neurofibromatosis, once known as Elephant Man's disease; and Marfan syndrome, a disorder marked by very long arms, legs, fingers and toes. More recent studies have linked father's age to prostate and other cancers in their children.

Columbia University researchers showed that women whose partners are thirty-five or older have three times as many miscarriages as women with partners under twenty-five. This is true no matter what the woman's age is. And the research confirmed that older men—just like older women—are at increased risk of fathering children with Down syndrome.

As researchers cataloged these ills, they found themselves increasingly puzzled by what was going on. How could sperm deteriorate with a man's age if they were always newly made? Perhaps the problem was mutations in the sperm-making machinery; but no one could be sure. There the matter rested, until research into the causes of schizophrenia unexpectedly began to point to older fathers.

•

Dolores Malaspina was in college when her sister, Eileen, who was two years younger, began behaving in ways the family couldn't explain. At first, Malaspina recalls, Eileen seemed like she was going through the usual problems of adolescence. She stopped doing her chores on the weekends, even though she had always pitched in before. She was tired and seemed depressed. At the time, Malaspina and her parents were not terribly concerned. "Many people who turn out perfectly well have lots of symptoms and struggles and conflicts during adolescence," she said. Soon, however, Eileen's behavior became harder to overlook. Malaspina's mother would wake up at night and discover that Eileen had strung scarves all through the house and set rules for the rest of the family about where in the house it was okay to walk, and where it wasn't. By then, the conclusion was inescapable: Eileen had serious problems. Eileen was finally hospitalized for the first time during her last year of high school. She was soon diagnosed with schizophrenia.

This was in the early 1970s, when many psychiatrists believed that schizophrenia was caused by a dominant, overpowering mother who rejected her child. "The prevailing notion was that this was not a biological disorder," said Malaspina. Further, Eileen's doctors said, there was no treatment. The damage done by a schizophrenia-inducing mother was irreparable, and the family should "hang crepe"—that is, prepare for a funeral. "There was a sense she would never be well, that we should lock her up and throw away the key." Malaspina, too, was tortured over whether she'd done something to cause her sister's illness. "I would replay our childhood over and over again. I'd think about the time I didn't want her to play with my friends and me, or when she called me once and I hid behind a tree. I spent many years feeling horribly guilty about that, and I'm sure for my mother it was magnified a hundredfold."

While Eileen was deteriorating, Malaspina continued in college, where she studied environmental biology and then zoology in graduate school. Before finishing her Ph.D., she got married and left graduate school, taking a job at a drug company, where she drifted into research on substances that could alter brain chemistry. She was in the job for a while before she made the connection with her sister. "I was looking at molecules in the lab that might be related to psychosis," she said. "My sister had very bad psychosis." Such research was beginning to establish a biological basis for schizophrenia and would ultimately demolish the notion that it was caused by domineering mothers. Malaspina, who'd never accepted the advice about hanging crepe, began to wonder whether it might be possible to find a drug that could help her sister. She quit her job and went to medical school with a single goal in mind—curing schizophrenia.

When she finished medical school and her residency, Malaspina took a research job at Columbia University in New York, where she ran into the first of many puzzles about the disorder. People with schizophrenia, because they often have trouble functioning, are much less likely than others to marry and have children. If people with schizophrenia are not reproducing as much as people without it, the disease should eventually disappear from the population. But it hasn't; the incidence of schizophrenia in the population has remained constant at about 1 percent. While schizophrenia can run in families, it might come as a surprise to learn that most cases are what are called sporadic—they show up in people with no family history of schizophrenia.

While mothers had long been blamed for causing schizophrenia, the biological approach to the study of disease began to raise questions about fathers. The problem was this: the eggs in a woman's body age as she does. Even if a woman has children when she's young, her eggs are already a couple of decades old. It seems logical to wonder whether they deteriorate as she gets older; we know that most of the rest of our body parts get a little ragged with age.

But that's not quite the way biology works. The time that cells are most susceptible to genetic damage is when they're dividing. That's when genes are copied, and they're not always copied correctly. Mistakes can pop up. That explains why sperm can be more vulnerable than eggs. Because they are being continuously manufactured, genetic copying is going on all the time. So it's sperm—not eggs—that are most likely to contain genetic errors. Geneticists think it's that incessant copying and recopying that gives rise to the genetic errors that cause dwarfism, Marfan syndrome, and the other ailments associated with older fathers. Malaspina learned about this when she was in medical school. With her single-minded focus on schizophrenia, she began to wonder whether the recognized potential for genetic errors in fathers' sperm might be at least partly responsible for schizophrenia.

At Columbia, Malaspina learned about a unique research opportunity in Israel. During the 1960s and 1970s, all births in and around Jerusalem were recorded, along with information on the infants' families. And all those children received a battery of medical tests as young adults, because of Israel's military draft. "All Jewish individuals in the country have to report to the draft board, and there is a mandatory screening for intelligence, psychiatric conditions, medical conditions," said Abraham Reichenberg, a neuropsychologist at Mount Sinai School of Medicine in New York, who has worked with Malaspina in studies of this population. "It's done on practically everybody unless they're out of the country or have died." Because the records cover an entire population, the data is free from the biases that might creep in if researchers looked at, say, only people who'd graduated from college, or only those who went to see a doctor.

In 2001, Malaspina had looked at the whether the risk of schizophrenia increased in the children of older fathers, and she found that it did. It was the first large-scale study to link sporadic cases of schizophrenia to fathers' age, and most researchers didn't believe it. "We were absolutely convinced it was real, but other people didn't think it was," Malaspina said. "Everybody thought men who waited to have children must be different." That is, maybe these older fathers had some of the makings of schizophrenia themselves—not enough for the disease to be recognized, but enough that it took these men a little longer to get settled, married, and have children.

Other groups tried to repeat the study using other populations. In all these studies, researchers took a close look at whether there was anything at all about older fathers, other than their age, that could have increased the risk of schizophrenia in their children. The link with age only became clearer. "That result has been replicated at least seven times," said Robert K. Heinssen, the director of the schizophrenia research program at the National Institute of Mental Health (which has funded some of Malaspina's work). "We're talking about samples from Scandinavia, cohorts in the United States, Japan. This is not just a finding that pertains to Israeli citizens or people of Jewish background."

Excited about the potential of further studies in the Israeli population, Malaspina investigated whether father's age might have an effect on children's intelligence. Studies have shown that teenagers who later develop schizophrenia have slightly lower IQs than those who remain healthy. This time, Malaspina and Reichenberg combined information on the Israeli children with the medical and intelligence tests done on their parents. The children of older fathers showed a drop in nonverbal intelligence, measured by such tasks as remembering a series of numbers or solving visual problems. The supposition is that whatever is increasing the risk of schizophrenia might also be affecting brain pathways associated with intelligence.

The researchers knew that the draft-induction tests identified young men and women with autism, and they realized they could look at that, too, to see whether it was linked to fathers' age. "There are similarities between autism and schizophrenia—they both have very severe social deficits," said Reichenberg. "There was some reason to think similar risk factors might be involved." In 2006, he, Malaspina, and their colleagues published the report showing that the children of men forty or older were six times as likely as the kids of men under thirty to develop autism or a related disorder. That's the study I heard about the day after our son was born.

Autism spectrum disorders occurred at a rate of 6 in 10,000 in the children of the younger fathers, and 32 in 10,000 among the children of the older fathers. (That's closer to five times the risk, but statistical adjustments showed the risk was actually about six times higher in the offspring of the older dads.) In the children of fathers over fifty, the risk was 52 in 10,000.

Reichenberg interprets that as a very solid finding. The study couldn't absolutely rule out some effect of older mothers, but he was confident that it was the fathers who were responsible for the increased autism risk. He and Malaspina considered the same question that had been raised in connection with the schizophrenia studies: Would fathers who are a little socially isolated or aloof, with minor language deficits—whom we might think of as a little bit autistic—take longer to get married? If so, it would mean the autism risk was due to something different about the fathers—not their age.

There were a couple of arguments against that idea. First, the risk of autism rose smoothly with increasing age, through the thirties, forties, and fifties. If the risk of autism were somehow related to social or language problems in the fathers, it shouldn't track age so closely. Secondly, the same argument has been made about mothers, some of whom, like men, might be said to be a little bit autistic. But the researchers didn't find a clear link between mothers' age and the risk of autism. Reichenberg and Malaspina are convinced the link to older fathers is real. And so are many other researchers.

Their findings have since been repeated and extended in a variety of ways. For example, researchers have looked at the genetics of older fathers to try to figure out what it might be in their genes that adversely affects their children. Schizophrenia and autism have been linked to a genetic mutation called a copy number variant, in which a section of

DNA is mistakenly copied one or more extra times and inserted into the sequence, or a section is deleted. When male mice of various ages were bred with young female mice, data showed that the offspring of the older males were much more likely to have new mutations of this kind than were the offspring of younger males. These mutations might therefore be the link between older fathers and the increased risk of schizophrenia and autism in their children. More mutations lead to a higher incidence of illness.

But does the same thing happen in humans? Researchers collected genetic information on 3,443 patients with intellectual disabilities—delayed intellectual development, or problems with social skills or taking care of themselves. They found that most of the subjects with copy number variants had inherited them from their fathers, and the mutations were especially associated with older fathers.

Reichenberg, continuing his research on older fathers, bred female mice with older males, and again with younger males. Offspring of the older fathers engaged in less social interaction with other mice and were more reluctant to explore a new environment. These are among the kinds of behavior problems sometimes seen in psychiatric illnesses.

Malaspina asked Jay Gingrich, a psychiatrist and neuroscientist at Columbia who works with mice, to join her in looking at the offspring of older males. Gingrich can't ask his mice whether they're suffering delusions or hearing voices. But he can give them tests that are analogous to those that people with schizophrenia have difficulty passing. One such test is to gently drop a young mouse into the center of a box about the size of a cafeteria tray—a place he's never seen before—and measure how much he wanders. If he shivers and stays where he is, he's showing that he has a deficit in a part of the brain known to be affected in schizophrenia. When Gingrich ran the tests, the pups of older fathers were slower to explore these unfamiliar environments than the offspring of younger fathers.

Gingrich found the same kind of paternal-age-related decline using an entirely different test. This time he looked at how mice reacted when they were startled by a loud sound. Mice are like people—when they hear a loud noise, they jump. And there's more similarity than that: when either mice or people hear a soft sound before being startled by a loud noise, they don't jump as much at the noise. It's called pre-pulse inhibition: the soft pulse inhibits the reaction to the louder one. "It's abnormal in a number of neuropsychiatric disorders, including schizophrenia, autism, obsessive-compulsive disorders, and some of the others," Gingrich told me. And, he found, it was more likely to be abnormal in mice with older fathers. Indeed, Gingrich thought the finding was almost too good to be true, and he didn't believe it at first. It wasn't until he and a postdoctoral student, Maria Milekic, had collected data on about one hundred offspring of younger dads and another hundred pups of older dads that he was convinced that the results were correct.

"We think this is a major cause of sporadic schizophrenia," Malaspina said. That would make it a major cause of schizophrenia, period, because 80 percent of cases are sporadic (that is, not occurring in families with schizophrenia).

There has been much talk of an increase in autism in recent years. Some say it's a real increase; others say it's because doctors are looking more carefully for it and therefore finding more cases. I asked Reichenberg whether the increase in the number of older fathers could explain a rise in autism cases. "I think there is a true increase in autism, and advancing paternal age might help explain some of that increase. But there is no proof. There might be a lot of other risk factors that have been increasing over the years," he said.

The idea that the rise in autism is due to the growing number of older fathers got a tremendous boost in the summer of 2012, when the Icelandic geneticist Kári Stefánsson and his colleagues looked at the question. Stefánsson is the chief executive of deCODE Genetics, a company based in Reykjavík, which bases its research partly on genetic samples from 140,000 people in Iceland and a family tree of the entire Icelandic population going back a thousand years. They compared the gene sequences of seventy-eight couples and their children and found that fathers were far more likely to pass on new mutations to the children than were mothers. And the number of mutations fathers passed along rose exponentially with their age. A thirty-six-year-old man will pass on twice as many mutations as a twenty-year-old father, and a seventy-year-old father will pass on eight times as many. They also estimated that an Icelandic child born in 2011 would have more new mutations than a child born in 1960. During that time, the average age of Icelandic fathers rose from twenty-eight to thirty-three. Most of these mutations are harmless, but some were indeed linked to the rise in schizophrenia and autism in Iceland.

The results suggest a new answer to the nagging question of why autism seems to be on the rise. Stefánsson calculated how many new cases of autism could arise as the consequence of fathers becoming older, on average. The mutations that he found in the children of older fathers could be the cause of 20 to 30 percent of all cases of autism, a stunningly high percentage. Stefánsson's study brought the concerns about older fathers to the front pages and home pages of newspapers and websites around the world.

While researchers now generally accept the findings on older fathers, not everyone agrees on what those results mean. "I think it's very interesting work," said Daniel R. Weinberger, a psychiatrist and schizophrenia expert who directs the Lieber Institute for Brain Development in Baltimore. He accepts the finding that the incidence of schizophrenia is higher in the children of older fathers. But he doesn't buy Malaspina's speculation that this could be one of the most important causes of schizophrenia—because, he said, researchers know too little about which genes conspire to cause schizophrenia. "It's a seminal observation, but like many seminal observations, it doesn't identify a mechanism." Weinberger wants to know exactly how this happens before he can say what it means.

Malaspina has thought a lot about the mechanism. What happens to the sperm of men as they age that could give rise to these increased risks to their offspring? The first idea was that it was a classic kind of genetic mutation, as some research has suggested. But another possibility is an alteration in the epigenetics of fathers' genes. As we've seen, some genes have a stamp, or imprint, that marks them as originating in fathers or mothers. Malaspina hasn't yet proven it, but she now believes that as men grow older, they may develop defects in cellular machinery that stamps this code on the genes. It's these imprinting defects, she suspects, that give rise to the increased risk of schizophrenia, autism, and perhaps some of the other ailments related to the father's age. It's not possible to poke around in people's brains and see whether those with schizophrenia have errors in this imprinting. But that can be done in Gingrich's mice. He is examining imprinting in the mice's brain tissue, and he's betting he'll find errors there. That's precisely the kind of research that could address Weinberger's concerns about the mechanism responsible for increasing the incidence of schizophrenia in the children of older dads.

If the genetic culprits underpinning schizophrenia and autism are identified, that would represent a big jump in understanding the illnesses. "This is work that we will pursue and fund, because we're so eager to get the genetics worked out," explains Thomas R. Insel of the National Institute of Mental Health. "It's a very interesting observation." With persistence—and some luck—the research could lead to better treatments or even, one day, a cure for schizophrenia and autism.

Until that happens, nothing can be done to test for schizophrenia or autism the way that doctors routinely test the fetuses of older women for, say, Down syndrome. There is no prenatal test for either of them, and the other genetic disorders linked to father's age are so rare that it would be impractical to test older couples for all of them, even if tests were routinely available. Nor is it yet possible to analyze an older man's sperm to see whether he is at special risk of having a child with problems. The only thing doctors can do is tell older fathers about the risks so they can make informed decisions. But even that isn't happening. And that should change. Genetic counselors often don't mention it, because nothing can be done to reduce the risks. But some couples, upon hearing the risks, might decide not to have children. And they should certainly be given that option.

The American College of Medical Genetics notes the risks, and suggests only that older fathers should be told about the increased risk of Down syndrome. It does not suggest they be advised about the risks of schizophrenia or autism. Its statement concludes by saying that "prospective couples should receive individualized genetic counseling to address specific concerns." I interpret that to mean that if couples have a concern about the risks of older fatherhood, they should ask about that. But if they don't express a "specific concern," they probably won't be told.

That seems wrong to me. I called two past presidents of the American College of Medical Genetics, Charles J. Epstein and Marilyn C. Jones, and asked them if they could explain why this "don't ask—don't tell" policy made sense, especially considering the new findings. "My personal philosophy has been to be truthful with people and tell them what they want to know," Epstein told me. But "to put it out there every time somebody comes to you for counseling probably engenders more fear than light."

Why then all the fuss about Down syndrome in the children of older women, when the risks for the children of older fathers are about the same? "You bring up Down syndrome because you get sued if you don't," he said. "And there are options. You can go through prenatal diagnosis, you have the option to terminate." Epstein points out that the general rate of abnormalities of all kinds in newborns is about 2 to 4 percent. So even a 3 percent risk of schizophrenia in the children of men over fifty is not out of line with other risks. And it sounds less frightening when put this way: a fifty-year-old man has a 97 percent chance of having a child without schizophrenia.

Jones agreed with Epstein. "Paternal age is usually not addressed in counseling couples of advanced age because there is no simple test to address the risk," she said. "If there is nothing to offer a couple but increasing anxiety, many counselors and physicians do not bring the issue up." Arthur L. Caplan, director of medical ethics at New York University, doesn't buy the geneticists' hands-off approach. "They should be revealing information they have," he said. "Parents might want to prepare, or it can affect a future reproductive decision." It's particularly important that parents have all the information, he said, because "this influences the health of someone whom nobody else can speak up for— the child." Jones asked me what I would have done if I'd known about these risks when Elizabeth was pregnant with our son. The answer is: probably nothing. But I wish I'd been told.

Some researchers worry that the new findings on schizophrenia and autism are just the beginning of the problems that might one day be associated with older dads. "If there is one common disease that we know is associated with older biological fathers, we can safely assume there are more remaining to be discovered," noted Elliot S. Gershon, a psychiatrist at the University of Chicago. "The now-common practice by men and women to delay parenting until they are almost too old to become parents has led to numerous medical disasters. It has long been known that infertility is a problem when women delay parenting, as well as Down syndrome. Now we know children of men who delay parenting also can end up paying a medical price."

Herbert Y. Meltzer, a psychiatrist and widely recog-

nized schizophrenia expert at Northwestern University,
said he believes the risks for children of older fathers will
eventually be seen to be as significant as the risks facing
older mothers: "It's going to be more and more of an issue
to society," he said. "Schizophrenia is a terrible disease, and
anything that can be done to reduce it is terribly important."
According to Meltzer, women might want to think about
this when choosing partners to have children with, and men
might want to think about having sperm stored when they're
young.

One well-known schizophrenia researcher echoed this
concern, explaining that he was concerned about his son,
who just got married at forty-two. "I brought this to his attention, not to alarm him, but so he would be aware of it,"
he said. "He and his wife might want to accelerate their
own personal schedule for having children."

Malaspina doesn't think it's proper to tell older men
what to do. But even that neutral stance has gotten her
into trouble. "I don't discourage men of any age from having
a family. And I've gotten e-mail from people saying, 'How
dare you, don't you understand the suffering of these diseases?' I just say the risks to any child of a man at any age
are small." Malaspina does believe that men should be
aware of the risks and be able to make these judgments for
themselves. "Men should know that this is an issue, just as
women know it's an issue. Men and women have their
healthiest children in their twenties."

It's an issue Malaspina has dealt with herself. Having a
sister with schizophrenia, she faced a 3 percent risk of having
a child with schizophrenia—exactly the risk that I face with
our son. Despite that, she decided to have a child—a daughter who's now in college and headed for medical school.

The real problem, Malaspina said, is that we live in a world in which it's increasingly difficult for people to have children when they're younger. "We might provide more child care. We need to make it possible to have children and continue a career." In her field, it's routine for students to delay having children until after they finish their internships and residencies and can begin to earn a living— something that eats up most of their healthiest childbearing years. This was a concern when only women's age was thought to be an issue; now, with fathers' risks becoming clear, it's doubly important.

While much of the news for older fathers has not been good, researchers have found some instances in which older fathers' genes confer benefits on their children. The first I found quite dramatic and unexpected: the children of older fathers have a particular genetic characteristic associated with longer life. And so do their children—that is, the grandchildren of the older fathers. The likelihood of longer life extends across at least two generations. Kids who had older fathers—and whose grandfathers were also older when they had children—got a double hit of this benefit.

The genetic benefit we're talking about here is a change in what are called telomeres. These are caps on the ends of chromosomes that protect chromosomes from damage as they divide. In most of our tissues, telomeres shorten as we age, and that could explain some of the consequences of aging. The children of older fathers have telomeres that are longer than normal. And they then pass those longer telomeres on to their children, who have even longer telomeres. Longer telomeres predict health and long life, making this a rather remarkable gift of older fatherhood.

A second curious finding about the children of older fathers is that they can grow to be slightly taller and slimmer than the children of younger fathers. Children born to dads over age thirty were found to be almost an inch taller, on average, than those born to fathers under thirty. And they could have a lower risk of obesity in adulthood. However, the children also had lower levels of HDL cholesterol, the kind associated with lower risks of heart disease. So the children could have an increased risk of heart disease as adults. The problems associated with older fatherhood greatly outweigh any conceivable benefits, but the mixed picture suggests that we need to know a lot more about what is happening on a molecular level. Men may have biological clocks, but biology is complicated, and those clocks seem to keep erratic time.

A few years ago, Thomas Foote, a retired professor of creative writing at Evergreen State College in Olympia, Washington, wanted to find out more about how older fathers are dealing with their erratic clocks. He began collecting narratives from older dads, in which they talked about their experiences. (Foote and his wife had a son when he was sixty, and the boy suffers from Down syndrome.) Most were in their second marriages and had been encouraged by younger wives to have children. Most were surprised at how much they were enjoying being fathers. Many of those who'd had children in an earlier marriage felt that they had the chance to get it right this time, to correct mistakes they felt they'd made with their older children. And most said they were spending more time with their children and felt they had a more intimate relationship with them than they had had when they were young fathers.

This bittersweet experience of the joys and perils of older fatherhood struck many cultural commentators as a

kind of sweet revenge. Women have been grappling with
decisions about childbirth for decades. Fathers seemed im-
mune; they could continue to have children at any age, however wise or unwise that might be. The idea that fathers' age
might pose risks to children was unexpected—and disturbing. My wife and I had a second child after we knew about
the risks associated with older fathers. Both are now old
enough that we no longer have to worry about their risk of
autism. But we must wait years before we can assure ourselves that they've escaped the risk of schizophrenia. I don't
worry about it often, but I can't quite dismiss it either.

NINE

What Fathers Do

I grew up in a Detroit suburb of small, pumpkin-colored brick houses, each with a spindly young Norway pine tied to stakes in front and usually a kettle-shaped, three-legged barbecue and a concrete birdbath in the back.

Most of the fathers in the neighborhood worked in the auto plants or the parts makers and tool-and-die shops that supplied them. My father was one of them. He worked from 7:00 a.m. until 3:30 in the afternoon and was home by 4:00. We were, in many respects, a traditional family, in a traditional neighborhood, with one television, one car, and one dream—that my sister and I would go to college, something neither of my parents had done.

In another respect, however, we were quite different from any of the other families on our block. Early on, before any of the other mothers on the block started working outside their homes, my mother took a job working three nights a week as a temp at Ford. She and the other temps would show up after 5:00 p.m., when everyone else had gone home, and type memos and letters until 10:00 or 11:00 p.m., finishing the work the regular secretaries hadn't been able to get to.

She would leave for work when my father got home, and he'd make dinner for my sister and me. We'd watch television after dinner, or play "ghost," a game he invented, in which he'd turn off all the lights and jump out of some unexpected corner while my younger sister and I clung together, thrilled and terrified. (I didn't know it then, but as we've seen, it was precisely the kind of play that fathers are known for.)

My parents weren't trying to reinvent gender roles, demonstrate their commitment to marital equality or launch a social movement. They were trying to raise a family. They lived with my grandmother for two years after they got married, saving money for the down payment on the house where they raised my sister and me. As absurd as it now seems, they couldn't make the $65 monthly mortgage payments on the $13,000 house unless they both worked.

Of course, other mothers were taking part-time jobs outside their homes, then full-time jobs. And life for most American families was irrevocably being transformed. Now it is nearly impossible for a middle-class family to get by on one parent's income.

This was in the 1960s, and when we talk about the division of labor in the family, that's usually where we start. Taking a longer view might mean looking back to women's employment during World War II, or possibly even to the beginnings of the industrial era, when fathers left their homes for factories. But the division of labor in the family goes back much, much further than that. As far back as we can see into prehistoric time, fathers and mothers divided up the work of the family, each making different contributions to the children and to the family's economy and welfare.

It's also true, however, that the structure of the family has changed in more recent decades, with many more fathers now living apart from their families—a situation that has prompted ferocious debate over the problem of fatherlessness and how serious its consequences might be for children. Whatever we think about that, and opinions vary, fatherless families give us a different way of understanding what fathers do—by watching what happens when they are not there. First we'll look at what has been learned about what fathers do in their homes and for their families; and then we will take up the subject of fatherless families.

Speculation about the social behavior of humans before recorded history is difficult to prove or disprove; we might never know what happened. Yet division of labor according to gender "is a human universal," true in all cultures, says the Harvard anthropologist Richard Wrangham. That means it would have appeared at least sixty thousand years ago, before humans began to spread around the world and diversify into those different cultures. Wrangham has an intriguing view of how and why this happened.

I find Wrangham's work interesting, not only because it says a lot about fathers and their families, but also because it forces us to take a long view of human family life and to reexamine what we believe to be true. For Wrangham, it starts with the discovery of fire. To learn more about how the gender division might have arisen, Wrangham, like Barry Hewlett and others, relies on observations of modern-day hunter-gatherers. In Wrangham's case, it's the Hadza tribe of northern Tanzania. In the morning, Hadza women take their babies and older children with them in search of a tuber called *ekwa*, a mainstay of their diet. They spend a few hours collecting enough for the day. Then they break briefly for lunch—a lovely spread of baked ekwa—and head back to camp, each carrying thirty pounds of the tubers. The men leave camp in the morning with bows and arrows, seeking food for the evening meal. Some come back with meat, some with honey, and some with nothing.

One of the things that's notable here is not only the kind of work men and women do, but the kind of food they collect. Each has different items on his or her shopping list. Women generally provide the staples and men the delicacies. One of the other notable features of their lives is that they pool their resources and share everything. This might not seem terribly surprising to us, but it is quite unusual: humans are the only primates in which adults share food. "Plenty of primates, such as gibbons and gorillas, have family groups," Wrangham writes. "Females and males in those species spend all day together, are nice to each other, and bring up their offspring together, but, unlike people, the adults never give each other food."

We've attached all kinds of importance to the sharing and division of labor in human families. The sociologist Émile Durkheim thought it promoted moral behavior by "creating a bond within the family." Some scholars thought it must have encouraged the evolution of intelligence and cooperation. One pair of anthropologists called the sexual division of labor the "true watershed for differentiating ape from human lifeways." Wrangham agrees that the division of labor is important, but he places more importance on another crucial development that accompanies it: cooking. Great apes spend half of their time chewing, because the rough, raw foods they eat—mostly ripe fruit, often with inedible pulp or seeds—require serious mastication before they can be swallowed and digested. If we ate the same raw foods that gorillas eat, we would have to spend about 40 percent of our day chewing—nearly half of our waking hours. If a hunter had to spend five hours eating every day, he wouldn't have enough time to hunt. Cooked food is softer and easier to eat, so men can eat more quickly. Cooking, Wrangham argues, extended the workday. It freed men to hunt and thus played a critical role in the sexual division of labor. Fire not only shortened the time it took to eat; it also enabled returning hunters to eat after dark, extending the useful amount of time in the day. The hunter could pursue game until dusk and still be able to eat after returning to the family camp. That was good for everyone, women and children included. But it was particularly good, Wrangham notes, for the men. Women cooked for them every night. The reason men got such a good deal, he suspects, is that they bullied women into it. It was "a primitive protection racket in which husbands used their bonds with other men in the community to protect their wives from being robbed, and women returned the favor by preparing their husbands' meals," Wrangham writes.

Researchers have looked for exceptions to this division of labor, but they haven't found many. A study published in the 1970s looked at cooking and other family activities in 185 different cultures. It found that women did the cooking in 98 percent of those societies. That's not the kind of study that's likely to be repeated, but there's no reason to think there has been any substantial change in the decades since. Even in the rare communities in which women did not do all the cooking, men cooked only for the community; women still cooked household meals. And the authors found one small exception in some of the groups: men often liked to cook meat. (It seems that men who like to barbecue are not a modern invention or an American one but just the latest example of a widespread human practice.)

Wrangham struggled to find one community, one tiny slice of humanity anywhere, that broke this pattern. He found studies by the anthropologist Maria Lepowsky of the people of Vanatinai, an island in the South Pacific. "Life was indeed very good for women," Wrangham writes. "Both sexes could host feasts . . . raise pigs, hunt, fish, participate in warfare, own and inherit land," and so forth. It was, in many respects, a fascinating example of equality of the sexes. Yet women still did all the cooking and dishwashing, fetched the water, and cleaned up pig droppings.

What's remarkable is that this arrangement didn't fall by the wayside somewhere during the course of history. American families in split-level houses or high-rise apartments don't have a lot in common with forest-dwelling hunter-gatherers, but both have organized their households in roughly the same way. "Cooking brought huge nutritional benefits," Wrangham writes. "But it also trapped women into a newly subservient role enforced by male-dominated culture . . . It is not a pretty picture."

Not everyone agrees with Wrangham's cooking hypothesis. For one thing, there is a problem with the timing. Wrangham believes the cooking of food began during the time of *Homo erectus*, a human ancestor that lived between 1.6 million and 1.9 million years ago. It had a much larger brain than *Homo habilis*, which came before, and in Wrangham's view that vast increase in brain size was likely due to the adoption of cooking. The transition to a larger brain occurred at the same time that the size of human teeth was decreasing, another sign that cooking had arrived, because cooked food is easier to chew. The problem is that there is little evidence that humans had discovered fire that long ago. C. Loring Brace, an anthropologist at the University of Michigan, notes that Neanderthals developed cooking 200,000 years ago, nowhere near as far back in time as Wrangham's theory requires. The larger brain and smaller teeth could have been due to a change in diet, not to cooking. Despite the criticism, Wrangham's theory is compelling, and it adds an important evolutionary component to a discussion of gender roles in the contemporary family, where this division of labor persists.

It continued with the arrival of farming, some 10,000 years ago. Men tended the fields and women prepared the food. Women likewise provided most of the child care. The division of labor survived the establishment of the first nation-states about 5,000 years ago. None of this is to argue that we're stuck with the household division of labor that arose in prehistoric times. There is no evolutionary argument that women must do the cooking. The point is that if we want to alter the way work is divided in the family, it's helpful to know that the current arrangement did not arise with our parents, our grandparents, or their parents. It's been entrenched far longer than that. Our gender roles have been with us for quite some time.

Not too many discussions of the roles of mothers and fathers in chores and child care begin with this long view. But if we want to learn something about fatherhood, we should look at how fathers were shaped during the living situations that characterized human history for hundreds of thousands of years—almost all of human existence. The rise of farming, nation-states, and factories each in turn forced dramatic changes on family life. For most of human history, fathers were responsible for protecting their children and for teaching them the things they needed to know to survive and prosper. Because that was true for so many millennia, fathers adapted to those demands, which became a matter of routine.

In that long prehistoric era, fathers taught their children how to work. Their children watched them work and often worked with them. Now children often instruct their fathers, showing them how to use their phones and computers. Cultural traditions handed down from fathers to children now compete with pop culture, which children often introduce to their parents. We no longer judge fathers exclusively on their ability to protect and educate their children, because we've turned those jobs over to the state. Instead, we judge fathers on their economic contributions to their families and on their caregiving. Fathers now earn the money they need to have someone else teach their children.

Changes in work and family life in the United States have accelerated during the past fifty years, in what is now a familiar trend. In 1965, 42 percent of women sixteen to sixty-four were employed. The same was true for 85 percent of men, more than twice the percentage of women. Women's employment rose through the rest of the twentieth century, peaking at 68 percent in 2000 before dropping back to 62 percent in 2011, mostly because of the recession. While women's employment was rising, men's was falling through 2011, when it stood at 71 percent.

But the difference in the trends for mothers and fathers is even greater than those numbers suggest. During that same period, from 1965 to 2011, the time that men spent at work fell from 42 hours per week to an average of about 37 hours per week. For mothers, the trend once again went in the opposite direction. They worked for pay an average of 8.4 hours a week in 1965 and 21.4 hours a week in 2011. In addition, fathers *and* mothers have both increased the time they spend with children. For fathers, the figure has nearly tripled, from 2.5 hours per week in 1965 to 7.3 hours. Mothers' time with children has increased slightly and is now 13.5 hours per week—nearly twice that of fathers.

Mothers spend more time at housework and child care than fathers do, a gap that we're familiar with. But when all the hours that men and women work inside and outside the home are put together, there is a surprising convergence: Fathers spend 54.2 hours per week working, counting paid and unpaid work. Mothers spend 52.7 hours per week in paid and unpaid work. So while discrepancies and differences remain, mothers and fathers are working roughly the same amount. Both mothers and fathers were working about three hours per week more in 2011 than they were in 1965.

Ellen Galinsky and her colleagues at the Families and Work Institute have found that men experience more conflict between work and family than women, a surprising finding considering that most of the discussion about work and family has centered around women. This is a big change. According to surveys of a national sample of men and women in 2009, 49 percent of men reported work-family conflicts, up from 34 percent in 1977. Men surpassed women, among whom 43 percent reported such conflicts in 2009. This doesn't mean that men have a monopoly on work-family conflicts. But it does mean that women no longer do.

A comparison with other countries makes that point. Americans work longer hours than many other people in developed countries, including Japan, where there is a word for "death by overwork"—*karoshi*. The United States is the only country out of thirty leading democracies that does not have laws protecting workers' paid maternity leave. Even unpaid leave is available to only about half of U.S. workers. Many Americans do not get paid sick days and can be forced to work overtime without any limits.

Why have work-family conflicts increased for fathers while remaining relatively steady for mothers? Many men say they feel they're being pushed harder at work, while their wages stagnate and the boundaries between work and family life are blurring. The situation is particularly difficult for fathers. Interestingly, they work significantly *more* hours per week than men without children. You might expect the reverse, but fathers say they work longer because the extra money is important for their families. The problem of work-family conflict is worst for men who believe flexibility will hurt their chances of advancement, and whose superiors make it difficult for them to respond to family emergencies and change their schedules on short notice. Men face an impossible ideal, a "male mystique" that puts demands on fathers that they can't possibly meet, Galinsky says. Men, in other words, like women, are now experiencing the pressure to have it all.

Galinsky thinks this situation can be changed, but only if change occurs "at all levels—from individuals' attitudes about work and family to effective workplace design and cultural change that dispel the mystiques for both men and women." The new male mystique, she says, "is harming men much in the ways that the feminine mystique harmed women."

The difficulty that fathers face trying to fulfill what they see as their responsibilities at work and at home generally turns out to be greater than they expect. During the third trimester of pregnancy, men and women both say that they expect women to be responsible for more of the baby care than fathers. But when their babies are six months old and they are asked again about the division of labor, most say mothers are doing even more than they had anticipated— and fathers are doing even less. The need for men's earnings to support the family often pushes couples in this direction, and fathers are often uncomfortable with it. A father in one study expressed frustration that his wages didn't seem to "count" as a contribution to the family as much as he thought they should. His wife's friends, he said, sometimes ask her why he doesn't spend more time with the baby. "Man, I'm looking after [my daughter] six days a week, ten hours a day, busting my ass at the plant," he said.

One consequence of the work-family conflict, according to Annette Lareau, a sociologist at the University of Pennsylvania, is that some men are indeed strangely detached from their families. Lareau and her team made repeated visits to families with kids in the third and fourth grades and interviewed the parents and children to try to determine the role of fathers in those families. They soon learned that interviewing the fathers was going to be more difficult than they'd anticipated: the men just didn't know much about the details of family life, even if they spent a lot of time with their families. Lareau found that fathers "were a powerful presence in the household" who "provided affection, humor, and advice to their children." But they had a hard time answering some simple questions, and they said they often relied on what their wives had told them. In one interview, a father is shown a list of children in his son's class and asked which parents he knows. He says that some of the names sound familiar, but he isn't sure. Referring to his wife, he said, "Harriet could tell me the ones I know." It wasn't that he didn't know the families; he simply couldn't remember exactly who was who.

Despite these lapses, which occurred frequently among the fathers in her study, Lareau found that fathers were not only important in family life, they *dominated* their families. "Fathers added color, fun, informality and 'accent' to family life. Mothers were likely to worry, chastise, and punish. Fathers were playful . . . We were repeatedly struck by the ways in which the fathers who participated in our study enlivened and lightened the tone of family life." Fathers also collaborated with mothers in teaching their children what Lareau calls "life skills" that wouldn't necessarily be taught in school. Fathers stressed the importance of masculinity and physical prowess, and they showed particular interest in children's athletic development over the kids' school, homework, and friendships. Fathers also taught their children— especially boys—how to fix things.

Fathers also grapple with social attitudes that suggest that stay-at-home fathers can't provide the same quality of parenting that stay-at-home mothers do. Victoria Brescoll and her colleagues at the Yale School of Management have collected attitudes on parenting and found significant stigma associated with nontraditional roles. With more women working, you might think that women who stay at home aren't viewed as favorably as those who are employed, but Brescoll found otherwise. Stay-at-home mothers and working fathers were viewed more favorably by the families in her studies than working mothers and stay-at-home dads. This could explain why many fathers take only some of their paternity leave (if they're lucky enough to get any) or don't take it at all; for men there is still a stigma associated with staying at home with children—even temporarily.

Furthermore, the participants in her study didn't express any embarrassment or hesitation over these views, which suggests "that these biases or beliefs about stay-at-home dads and working moms are strong, and people don't feel bad about having the bias," she said. "If a father is a breadwinner and they're both working, and he's pitching in as much as she is, I think people would feel that's fine, because he's still making money." But if he's working part time and doing a lot of child care, people will judge him. The stereotypes remain; the first thing fathers have to do is to prove they can support the family financially.

Many attitudes and circumstances influence what a father does at home, but one of the most important is what's often called maternal gatekeeping—the controversial notion that women might block men's participation in housework and child care. Despite the move of more mothers to the workplace and greater interest among men in spending time with their children, mothers still do more of the housework and child care in the home. It could be that mothers and fathers are still partly ensnared in traditional views of gender roles. But there is reason, according to some researchers, to think that some mothers are preventing fathers from becoming more involved.

The roots of this dynamic extend back to the beginning of the twentieth century, when men began to work in factories and women became the experts in running the home. This breakdown of roles was still in place in the 1960s, when the feminist movement began to challenge these gender stereotypes. But the movement of women into the work-place and the trend toward fathers doing more at home have not changed the fact that women still do more of the work at home. "Some women both cherish and resent being the primary caregiver and feel both relieved and displaced by paternal involvement," one study concluded. Many mothers say they would like fathers to be more involved in child care, but some reports suggest that as many as 60 to 80 percent of mothers *do not* want their husbands to be more involved in child rearing.

Accusing women of keeping fathers out of family life is a serious charge, because it blames women for undermining their own progress toward a more reasonable division of family responsibilities during a time of dramatic change in the workplace. But there is evidence to support it. And some of the best evidence comes from Sarah J. Schoppe-Sullivan of Ohio State University and her colleagues.

They asked ninety-seven couples about their child-rearing beliefs before their first child was born, surveying them afterward, and observing them at home with their new babies. Schoppe-Sullivan found that mothers did play important roles in both encouraging and curtailing fathers' involvement. And their gatekeeping was a powerful force: even fathers who wanted to be involved with their kids of-ten drifted away in the face of persistent maternal criticism. Encouragement clearly proved to have a more powerful ef-fect on fathers. "Mothers can close the gate, but they can also open the gate," Schoppe-Sullivan said.

When she asked couples what kind of parents they wanted to be and later compared that to the kind of par-ents they became, she found a poignant discord. Some of the couples eagerly looked forward to sharing parenting—

but it didn't happen. The roles become more traditional. Mothers generally assumed the larger role, and both were disappointed with that outcome. These mothers, Schoppe-Sullivan explained, are not consciously trying to shut fathers out. It's just something that happens. And one important reason is that life after the arrival of a newborn often doesn't meet parents' expectations.

In addition to helping explain how fathers behave with their kids, the findings say something more broadly about marital satisfaction. Many parents report a downward spiral in marital satisfaction after their children are born, and the division of household labor and chores can undergo a major shift. If their arrangement was working well before the birth, it might suddenly deteriorate in the face of all the new responsibilities, from taking care of a larger pile of laundry to arranging for child care.

Many parents plan to do a better job of sharing responsibilities after the baby is born, but not all of them succeed. Parents lose much of the time they had spent together before the baby—no more running out to catch a movie or a drink after work, no more lingering over a relaxing dinner. Dinner is now more likely to be something you try to cook, eat, and clean up before you collapse into bed, exhausted from work and caring for the children. These things—some of them trivial, others substantial—can shake the foundation of a marriage. And this is one of the biggest threats to committed and involved fatherhood.

Throughout this book, we have tried to determine what fathers contribute to their families by looking closely at families through the eyes of anthropologists, geneticists, and psychologists, among others. They have told us a lot about fatherhood. But there is an entirely different way to look for fathers' contributions—and that is to look at families in which the fathers are absent. Some authorities believe this is a severe social problem with harsh consequences for children. Others suggest that fatherlessness, as it's often awkwardly called, is not nearly so harmful.

The first question we should ask about father absence is: How widespread *is* it? I found the answers to be shocking, almost unbelievable. Depending on which study you look at, between one-quarter and one-half of the American children of divorced parents never, or almost never, see their fathers. One-third of all children are born to parents who aren't married, up from 6 percent in 1960. Some of those couples will stay together, but many won't.

All the current figures are far higher than they were only a few decades ago. In 1960, only 11 percent of U.S. children lived apart from their fathers. By 2010, that figure had climbed to 27 percent. (The share of children living apart from their mothers rose from 4 percent to 8 percent.) It's no surprise that fathers who live apart from their children spend far less time sharing meals, helping with homework, and playing. About 40 percent of nonresident fathers say they are in touch with their children several times a week by e-mail or phone. One in five say they visit more than once a week, and 29 percent see them at least once a month.

Fewer fathers are living with or are in touch with their children now than at any time since the United States began keeping relatively reliable statistics. Those fathers who are separated, divorced, or never married—but who see their children regularly—are not likely to be involved in monitoring them or setting and enforcing rules, meaning they are not really playing a parental role. And we've made little progress in understanding why so many fathers live apart from their families—and what we can and should do to change this.

In chapter 6, I discussed a study of hunter-gatherer groups that found that fathers had little or no effect on mortality rates among their children. Researchers have also looked at the consequences of father absence in the United States and have come to a different conclusion. One study done in the state of Georgia found that children born to unmarried mothers with no father listed on the birth certificate were two and a half times more likely to die within a year of birth as children born to married women who listed a father. Unmarried mothers are more likely than other mothers to live in poverty, so it could be primarily economic circumstances, rather than fathers' absence, that are responsible for the additional deaths (although these two are often linked). But when researchers did an analysis that eliminated some of the economic factors, they still found that children with no father on their birth certificates were twice as likely to die as children whose fathers were named.

Multiple studies suggest that fatherlessness is a major contributor to crime and juvenile delinquency; premature sexuality and out-of-wedlock births to teenagers; deteriorating educational achievement; depression, substance abuse, and alienation among adolescents; and the growing number of women and children in poverty. That list comes from David Popenoe of Rutgers University, who says the decline of fatherhood "is a major force behind many of the most disturbing problems that plague American society."

The National Fatherhood Initiative, an organization founded to study fatherlessness and encourage father involvement, has looked closely at some of the data linking fatherlessness to adverse consequences for children. With regard to delinquency, it has found that the closer adolescents feel to their fathers, the less likely they will be to engage in delinquent behavior—such as stealing, running away, disorderly conduct, violence, and the use of weapons. Relationships with mothers are important, too, but the emphasis on fathers is especially so in families in which the fathers live apart. The NFI has also looked at the evidence linking father-adolescent relationships with drug abuse, and came to similar conclusions. The influence of peers was a factor in drug use, but adolescents who had good relationships with their parents had less need to seek outside relationships that could lead to risky behavior.

Popenoe says the evidence is overwhelming that "on the whole, two parents—a father and a mother—are better for the child than one parent." He acknowledges exceptions, which include disastrous two-parent families and devoted single parents who can raise healthy, fulfilled children. But the exceptions don't invalidate the rule. Popenoe believes that in gay and lesbian couples, one usually fills the "male" role and the other the "female," but he acknowledges there isn't enough data on child outcomes in these families to know how much that matters.

The most important and immediate consequence of fatherlessness, in his view, is the loss of economic resources. When families divorce, household income falls and expenses rise. Two homes cost more than one, and divorce does not come with an increase in parents' wages.

It's not surprising that many other researchers have criticized this point of view. Divorce and fathers' absence often follow an extended period of conflict between the parents, and it's possible that the *conflict*, not the father's absence, is responsible for some of the children's problems. And separated families may be different in some other, unknown way from families that stay together.

Families with unmarried parents often defy expectations, says Sara S. McLanahan of Princeton University, who studies such families. "One of the surprises was how attached these parents really are to each other," McLanahan told me. But many did not live together. "These people are not rejecting marriage; they're hoping to get married, and the fathers are very involved." They help the mothers through pregnancy and come to the hospital for the birth. But their resources are limited. They are often very poor. About half of the fathers had been incarcerated before the birth of their child. And only about one third of these couples are together five years later. "Parents are breaking up and repartnering. There is a lot of instability. And they are having children with new partners." And the study shows that the children in these families are not doing as well as children in stable families.

McLanahan and one of her colleagues, Marcia J. Carlson of the University of Wisconsin–Madison, have looked at what might be done to encourage fathers in poor families to become more involved with their children. Efforts to prevent unwanted pregnancy among unmarried women, especially teens, were only partly successful. Efforts to encourage greater father involvement by focusing on increasing absent fathers' child-support payments did not work out so well. The problem was that the absent fathers often didn't have the resources to make the payments. And programs to boost fathers' emotional involvement with their children also largely failed, but those that encourage involvement at the time of a child's birth looked promising.

"We're realizing that the mother-father relationship is crucial," Carlson told me. As we saw earlier, maternal gate-keeping is an important issue to consider. "The more nuanced understanding now is that the mom can encourage the dad or discourage the dad, and it probably has a lot to do with how she perceives him as a guy. The more a mother and father cooperate and can trust each other, the more the nonresident father stays involved." Father involvement can also be influenced by whether a mother has a new partner—a social father, as "for a lot of kids, the biological father isn't the last father they're going to have," she said. And sometimes "the social father tends to be as involved as the biological father." Carlson believes that worries about father absence and its harmful consequences for children are justified. Kids without fathers or father figures playing an active role in their lives face greater risks.

Once again, the laboratory animals nicely complement the work done with human families. In this case, the basic research has helped to explain *why* father absence makes a difference to children. Poverty in children might actually alter the wiring of their brains.

Katharina Braun and her colleagues in Germany looked at the brains of rodents found in Chile called degus, which have complex families and social structures and engage in play. Male degus are exemplary fathers: they invest a lot in their pups and spend more time with them as they grow up, while the mother gradually withdraws. The father huddles with the pups, licks and grooms them, and carries them on his back. And degus have a curious feature that makes them interesting for father research: when fathers are absent, the mothers don't compensate by spending more time with the pups. So it's fair to assume that the pups raised by a single mother "are in fact partly emotionally deprived," Braun and her colleagues have found. Whatever they could find out about that emotional deprivation in degus could point the way toward identifying similar deprivation in human subjects.

Previous studies with other rodents had shown that separation from a mother or a father could produce wiring changes in the brains of their pups, especially in the anterior cingulate cortex, a part of the brain's frontal cortex involved in emotions and thinking, as well as communication and social interactions. Braun and her team wanted to see if the absence of a father could rewire that anterior cingulate cortex in their pups. When they raised pups without fathers and examined their brains under the microscope, they found that their suspicions were correct: the father-deprived degu pups had fewer synapses, or connections, in that portion of the cortex.

As I've noted, the separation of a human father from his family can also lead to poverty, and it's becoming clear that poverty itself can produce changes in the frontal cortex. Mark M. Kishiyama at the University of California, Berkeley, looked at twenty-six children seven to twelve years old and assessed their brains' electrical activity as they looked at a variety of images on a computer screen. Thirteen of the children—boys and girls from different ethnic groups— were from families with college-educated parents and a mean annual family income of $96,157. The other thirteen were from families without college-educated parents and with a mean annual income of $27,192. The children were also given a battery of neuropsychological tests to measure their competence in such things as memory and proficiency in language. Indeed, the researchers found that the workings of the prefrontal cortex were altered in the poor children, in a pattern resembling what happens to people with frontal-cortex damage.

When we put all this together, we can make a strong case that the absence of a father in a family can have devastating consequences for children. Many children do well, of course, without fathers in their homes. We all know children who grew up in difficult circumstances but now live rich and re-warding lives. Not all of them grow up to be the president of the United States, but Barack Obama is an example of what can be achieved by a child who grew up without a father but managed to overcome it.

Some researchers who study fathers have concluded that while they have become convinced that involved fa-thers are important for children, they are not *essential*. I doubt that many of them want to rewind the tape to the 1950s, with fathers as breadwinners—who were not en-couraged to be involved dads—and mothers as homemak-ers. The economic pressures that have driven many women into the workforce have created an opportunity for fathers to be far more involved with their children than they have been in the past.

When my children from my first marriage were young, I lived in New Jersey and commuted to a demanding job at the Associated Press in Rockefeller Center. I boarded a train before 7:00 a.m., and if a story wasn't breaking late in the day, I got home at 6:30 p.m., with just enough time to ask them about their day and read to them before they went to bed. Now my wife and I both work at home, and I can adjust my schedule to spend much more time with my children. I'm glad to know my involvement is a good thing. But that's not why I spend time with my kids. I do it because I like it.

Afterword: Fathers Matter

During the time that I was researching and writing *Do Fathers Matter?*, I met many parents who wanted to know more about what I was finding out. Casual conversations, sometimes with people I'd just met, would turn into surprisingly personal discussions about fathers, about our own fathers, and about our children. One single mother of twins asked me, only half jokingly, "What do I need to know?"

Sometimes the stories were very moving, as in the case of one woman who offered to tell me about the unusual experience she'd had with her family. "I never knew my birth father," she told me. Her parents had had only "a very brief relationship that ultimately resulted in me," she said. When she was too young to go find her father, her mother never made any attempt to introduce them. When she was old enough to go after him herself, she was resentful that he had never come looking for her. "I never wanted to meet him. I was very much of the opinion that he was the adult, and it was his responsibility to seek me out. He never did."

Later, when she thought about having children, though, she began to wonder about him—where he was, what he was doing, and who his relatives might be, because they would be her relatives, too, of course. She tracked him down online, where she discovered that he had died just a few months earlier. She also learned that he and his family had lived in the same town as she did when she was growing up. She decided to get in touch with her newly discovered relatives.

"I had cousins who knew people I went to school with. I had a new set of aunts and uncles who knew my other set of aunts and uncles. And there I was, finally wanting to know my real father, with no hope of ever doing so . . . except through his family." She told me that as a child, she had been an A student with shabby clothes—a teacher's pet who got picked on for being "a little too chubby and a little too smart."

She went on to earn a Ph.D., after some difficult emotional crises, and is now a scientist and a journalist. But, she says, "I'll never really know what it's like to have a father. When I read about fathers being a big influence in the development of confidence or persistence or strength or grit, I'll always wonder what I would have been like with a father." The father she never knew clearly matters in her life, even though she had rejected the idea of connecting with him earlier. The relatives she is now coming to know say that they see a lot of him in her.

Another woman, Alana, is the daughter of a sperm donor whose identity and whereabouts she tried to discover, only to find that her birth father was untraceable. When she told a friend that she hoped to someday meet a man with whom she could have kids, the friend replied, "You don't have to have a man in your life to have children." Alana was stung by the response. Her mother had decided to have a child without a man in her life, and that decision had devastated Alana. After giving the matter some thought, she wrote a response to her friend's remark:

"As a matter of fact, you *do* need a man to have a child—and a woman too! Kids (like me!) eventually grow brains and realize that they've been suckered out of a major, *major* requisite for happiness." She refers to sperm donation as "deliberate spiritual robbery." Alana desperately wants to know something about her biological heritage. It's not just that she wishes she had known her father; it's that knowing him would be knowing more about who *she* is. A talented musician, Alana told me she hopes to become famous enough through her music that one day her father will spot her face on an album cover, see that she resembles him, and recognize that she must be his daughter. And that he will get in touch.

These stories are reminders of the importance of fathers in people's lives. As a father myself, I might be accused of having a one-sided point of view of the significance of fathers. But conversations with these women and with countless men told me that I am not alone in believing that fathers are important. These two women I've described feel a powerful sense of loss, a loss that some grief experts call ambiguous loss. Never having known their fathers, or having known what it's like to grow up with a father in their families, they don't know exactly what they've lost, but they feel the pain and the yearning.

As both a journalist and a father, I've watched as the research on fatherhood has unfolded over the past decade. The science is affirming what many fathers and their families believe. Yet the message has only gradually begun to reach the world outside laboratories and universities. While fathers are now very much a part of our discussions of family life, we are still slow to accept men and women as equal parents.

One place where this can be plainly seen is in the courts, where family issues are often stripped to their barest

essentials. Research on fathers has produced scarcely a ripple there. Heartbreaking decisions are made hundreds of
times every day by judges who seem to know nothing about
modern notions of fatherhood. We might have expected
this sort of ignorance in the early days of research on
fatherhood, and, indeed, it's easy to find. One striking example occurred in 1988, when a judge in Detroit was considering a case in which a father was seeking custody of his
daughter, then twenty-two months old. Experts testified
that the girl had a closer relationship with her father than
with her mother and that he had been her primary caretaker. Speaking from the bench, the judge sputtered, "I
don't buy it. I don't buy it. I don't buy that the father is better for a twenty-two-month-old girl than the mother. And I
can't swallow it. I'm going to vomit on it . . . I don't care how
good a father [he is]."

The attitude persists. As recently as the fall of 2012, the
family law newsletter of the National Organization for
Women (NOW) denounced joint custody between mothers
and fathers, suggesting that fathers sought joint custody
only to reduce their child support payments. "The fathers'
custody activists claim that both legal and physical joint
custody is in the best interest of the child. But it is no coincidence that joint custody drastically reduces the father's
child support payments and other financial obligations,"
the newsletter said. "In reality, after joint custody is agreed
to or ordered by the court, many mothers often have the
child or children most of the time, while the reduced child
support payment from the father negatively impacts the
mother's ability to support the child or children." I'm sure
that this is true some of the time. But nowhere here does
the newsletter concede that some fathers might seek joint
custody because they want to spend more time with their

children. Nor do the authors seem to be aware that involvement of fathers in their children's lives is important. Instead, the newsletter links to a website that features a list of the "myths and facts" related to fatherhood and family law. Myth number one? "A father's involvement is crucial for the well-being of a child."

Similar anti-father sentiments have arisen as some state legislatures have considered shared-parenting bills, in which fathers and mothers would have joint custody unless circumstances dictated otherwise. When the New York State legislature considered such a bill in 2006, NOW–New York State argued strongly against more father involvement. "If a person is not involved in the lives of his or her children during the marriage, why would that involvement increase after divorce?" wrote Marcia A. Pappas, its president at the time. That's a reasonable question—in the case of the father Pappas was describing, the involvement probably wouldn't have increased. But the question presumes that all fathers are the same, and that none of them is involved in the lives of his children—which certainly isn't true.

The same dismissiveness of fathers is seen in advertising, too. Remember those commercials in which Huggies wanted to see if its diapers were tough enough to survive the ineptitude of fathers? "Put Huggies to the test!" the spots said. And how about the post on Clorox's website that read, "Like dogs or other house pets, new dads are filled with good intentions but lacking the judgment and fine motor skills to execute well"? Setting aside the question of whether dogs or gerbils are filled with good intentions, such ads are funny only if the people watching or reading them are comfortable with the idea that fathers are incompetent. Not all viewers found the spots amusing. Huggies dropped its commercials. Clorox saw the reaction to its commercial and, sensitive to the views of its potential customers, was quick to drop it.

Meanwhile, other companies are beginning to produce ads that paint fathers in a *positive* light—a relatively new development. In 2010, for instance, Subaru ran a series of commercials featuring fathers and kids, including one in which a worried father hands his car keys to a daughter who has just learned to drive. The viewer sees her as a teenager; when the father looks at her, he still sees her as his little girl. Tide and its fabric softener, Downy, produced a commercial that illustrates a father's role in play, in which the father does the laundry and plays "sheriff" with his daughter, who arrests him. "I got twenty minutes to life," he says in mock dismay. Unlike the commercials featuring fathers with poor fine-motor skills, this one shows a father who is competent and comfortable with his child.

That's what I would like to see more of. Fatherhood is about helping children become happy and healthy adults who are at ease in the world and prepared to become fathers or mothers themselves. We often say that doing what's best for our kids is more important than anything else we do. What's best for our kids should always include a role for fathers.

Part of what drove me to write this book was meeting my wife, creating a life with her, and getting the unexpected and overwhelming opportunity to take a second shot at raising kids. Has the research on fatherhood opened my eyes to a better way to be a father? In many ways, yes. Does that mean I'm getting it right?

I defer to my children on that.

Notes

INTRODUCTION: CLEANING OUT THE ATTIC

4 *When Alex Rodriguez*: George Vecsey, "Thrown by Life's Curveballs, a Star Missed the Signals," *New York Times*, Aug. 4, 2013, www.nytimes.com /2013/08/05/sports/baseball/bedeviled-by-lifes-curveballs-rodriguez -misses-the-guideposts.html?pagewanted=all.

6 *"the father is an almost irrelevant entity"*: Michael E. Lamb, ed., *The Role of the Father in Child Development*, 1st ed. (New York: Wiley, 1976), 1.

7 *"the interaction that at least some infants have"*: Ibid., 3–5.

8 *"clear survival value"*: Ibid., 7.

8 *fathers were excited about becoming parents*: Ibid., 25.

9 *whether treating depressed mothers might reduce*: Myrna M. Weissman et al., "Remissions in Maternal Depression and Child Psychopathology: A STAR*D-Child Report," *Journal of the American Medical Association* 295, no. 12 (2006): 1389–98.

10 *the experiment was over*: Lamb, *Role of the Father*, 1st ed., 29–30.

10 *even when fathers are included in research*: Kyle D. Pruett, *Fatherneed: Why Father Care Is as Essential as Mother Care for Your Child* (New York: Free Press, 2000), 6.

11 *This disregard of fathers*: Elizabeth H. Pleck and Joseph H. Pleck, "Fatherhood Ideals in the United States: Historical Dimensions," in *The Role of the Father in Child Development*, 3rd ed., edited by Michael E. Lamb (New York: Wiley, 1997), 42.

11 *Clorox published a post*: Josh Levs, "Amid Fury, Clorox Pulls Post Insulting New Dads," CNN.com, June 27, 2013, www.cnn.com/2013/06/27 /living/cnn-parents-dads-clorox.

14 *"companions, care providers, spouses"*: Michael E. Lamb, ed., *The Role of the Father in Child Development*, 4th ed. (Hoboken, NJ: Wiley, 2004), 3.

14 *"Although diametrically opposed"*: Ross D. Parke and Armin A. Brott, *Throwaway Dads: The Myths and Barriers That Keep Men from Being the Fathers They Want to Be* (Boston: Houghton Mifflin, 1999), 4–5.

15–16 *"We need to help all the mothers"*: Barack Obama, Father's Day Remarks (transcript), *New York Times*, June 15, 2008, www.nytimes.com /2008/06/15/us/politics/15text-obama.html?pagewanted=all.

1. THE ROOTS OF FATHERHOOD: PYGMIES, FINCHES, AND FAMINE

19 *Certain monogamous titi and night monkey fathers*: Sarah Blaffer Hrdy, *Mothers and Others: The Evolutionary Origins of Mutual Understanding* (Cambridge, MA: Harvard University Press, 2009), 88.

19 *Human fathers might not show*: Harriet J. Smith, *Parenting for Primates* (Cambridge, MA: Harvard University Press, 2006), 71. Hrdy, *Mothers and Others*, 161–64.

20 *But we have some hints, sifted from*: Barry S. Hewlett, *Intimate Fathers: The Nature and Context of Aka Pygmy Paternal Infant Care* (Ann Arbor: University of Michigan Press, 1991), 157–62.

21 *the increasing size of the human brain*: Richard Wrangham, *Catching Fire: How Cooking Made Us Human* (New York: Basic Books, 2009), 119.

21 *But being born earlier had a cost*: Hewlett, *Intimate Fathers*, 151–65.

21 *13 million calories' worth of breast milk*: Hrdy, *Mothers and Others*, 101.

22 *Agriculture was invented only*: Ibid., 73.

23 *The Aka's skill at foraging and hunting*: Hewlett, *Intimate Fathers*, 11–14.

23 *Aka infants are held almost constantly*: Ibid., 32.

24 *If an infant fusses or urinates*: Ibid., 33.

24 *Aka fathers spend 47 percent of their day*: Ibid., 126.

24 *part of dads' nights out*: Ibid., 140.

25 *a father named Yopo*: Ibid., 103–104.

25 *do a lot of their child care in the evenings*: Ibid., 89–90.

26 *"because they can communicate their love and concern"*: Ibid., 172.

27 *The first glimmer of this phenomenon*: Emily Anthes, "The Bad Daddy Factor," *Pacific Standard*, Dec. 10, 2010, www.psmag.com/health/the -bad-daddy-factor-25764.

28 *Swedish researchers were drawn to Överkalix*: L. O. Bygren et al., "Longevity Determined by Paternal Ancestors' Nutrition During Their Slow

Growth Period," *Acta Biotheoretica* 49 (2001): 53–59, http://depts.washing
ton.edu/lairdlab/pdfs/BygrenEtAl2001.pdf.

29 *historical records of harvests in Överkalix*: M. E. Pembrey et al., "Sex-
Specific, Male-Line Transgenerational Responses in Humans," *European Journal of Human Genetics* 14, no. 2 (2006): 159–66.

29 *mothers who overeat or are obese*: Sara Reardon, "Dad's Diet May Give
Children Diabetes," Science NOW, Oct. 20, 2010, http://news.science
mag.org/health/2010/10/dads-diet-may-give-children-diabetes.

30 *alterations in the workings of 642 genes*: Sheau-Fang Ng et al., "Chronic
High-Fat Diet in Fathers Programs Beta-Cell Dysfunction in Female
Rat Offspring," *Nature* 467 (2010): 963.

30 *fathers' high-fat diets had produced*: Michael K. Skinner, "Fathers' Nutritional Legacy," *Nature* 467 (2010): 922, www.bio.davidson.edu/genomics
/2011/Bio309_papers/Father_legacy_comm.pdf.

30 *feeding male mice a diet*: Benjamin R. Carone et al., "Paternally Induced
Transgenerational Environmental Reprogramming of Metabolic Gene
Expression in Mammals," *Cell* 143, no. 7 (2010): 1084–96, www.ncbi.nlm
.nih.gov/pmc/articles/PMC3039484.

31 *exposed adult male mice to chronic stress*: David M. Dietz et al., "Paternal
Transmission of Stress-Induced Pathologies," *Biological Psychiatry* 70,
no. 5 (2011): 408–14, www.ncbi.nlm.nih.gov/pmc/articles/PMC3217197.

31 *another example of the grandfather effect*: Lorena Saavedra-Rodríguez
and Larry A. Feig, "Chronic Social Instability Induces Anxiety and De-
fective Social Interactions Across Generations," *Biological Psychiatry*
73, no. 1 (2013): 44–53.

32 *increased startle response to the same odor*: Brian G. Dias and Kerry J.
Ressler, "Parental Olfactory Experience Influences Behavior and Neural
Structure in Subsequent Generations," *Nature Neuroscience*, Dec. 1,
2013, www.nature.com/neuro/journal/vaop/ncurrent/full/nn.3594.html.

32 *exposing lab rats to a fungicide*: Begley, "Sins of the Grandfathers,"
Newsweek.com, Oct. 30, 2010, http://mag.newsweek.com/2010/10/30/how
-your-experiences-change-your-sperm-and-eggs.html.

33 *they looked at large populations of male workers*: Tania A. Desrosiers
et al., "Paternal Occupation and Birth Defects: Findings from the National
Birth Defects Prevention Study," *Occupational and Environmental
Medicine* 69, no. 8 (2012): 534–42.

34 *I heard this story from*: James P. Curley, interview with the author,
Jan. 4, 2011.

2. CONCEPTION: THE GENETIC TUG-OF-WAR

41 *analysis of the history of the Y chromosome*: Nicholas Wade, "Genetic Maker of Men Is Diminished but Holding Its Ground, Researchers Say," *New York Times*, Feb. 22, 2012, www.nytimes.com/2012/02/23/science /y-chromosome-though-diminished-is-holding-its-ground.html.

42 *Surani was a young developmental biologist*: M. Azim Surani, interview with the author, Aug. 3, 2013; and Surani, interview with Alan Macfarlane, June 19, 2009, www.alanmacfarlane.com/DO/filmshow/surani1_fast .htm.

44 *Surani's colleagues didn't believe*: Ilona Miko, "Gregor Mendel and the Principles of Inheritance," *Nature Education* 1, no. 1 (2008): 134, www .nature.com/scitable/topicpage/gregor-mendel-and-the-principles-of -inheritance-593.

45 *a direct challenge to this principle*: Ibid.

55 *the ability of the fetus to alter*: David Haig, "Genetic Conflicts in Human Pregnancy," *Quarterly Review of Biology* 68, no. 4 (1993): 495–532.

58 *discover the first imprinted gene*: Thomas M. DeChiara et al., "A Growth-Deficiency Phenotype in Heterozygous Mice Carrying an Insulin-like Growth Factor II Gene Disrupted by Targeting," *Nature* 345 (1990): 78; T. M. DeChiara et al., "Parental Imprinting of the Mouse Insulin-like Growth Factor II Gene," *Cell* 64, no. 4 (1991): 849–59.

59 *mothers' powerful counterweapon*: Bernhard Horsthemke, "Of Wolves and Men: The Role of Paternal Child Care in the Evolution of Genomic Imprinting," *European Journal of Human Genetics* 17, no. 3 (2009): 273–74, www.ncbi.nlm.nih.gov/pmc/articles/PMC2986180.

61 *explain the origins of some mental illnesses*: Christopher Badcock and Bernard Crespi, "Battle of the Sexes May Set the Brain," *Nature* 454 (2008): 1054.

64 *a cure . . . for Angelman syndrome*: Arthur L. Beaudet, "Angelman Syndrome: Drugs to Awaken a Paternal Gene," *Nature* 481 (2012): 150–52, www.uam.es/personal_pdi/ciencias/jmsierra/documents/Beaudet2012Nat .pdf.

3. PREGNANCY: HORMONES, DEPRESSION, AND THE FIRST FIGHT

68 *Two years after they married*: Carolyn Pape Cowan and Philip A. Cowan, *When Partners Become Parents: The Big Life Change for Couples* (New York: Basic Books, 1992), 1.

69 *The study included seventy-two couples*: Ibid., x.

70 *what happens to fathers during pregnancy*: Ibid., 52, 57, 53, 65, 67.

71 *"Almost every expectant father told us"*: Ibid., 65.

72 *enter school feeling loved and supported*: Kyle D. Pruett and Marsha Kline Pruett, *Partnership Parenting: How Men and Women Parent Differently—Why It Helps Your Kids and Can Strengthen Your Marriage* (New York: Da Capo, 2009), 22.

72 *did less of the family work at home*: Cowan and Cowan, *When Partners Become Parents*, 100.

72 *The changes that occur in men*: Ibid., 52.

73 *One of the key hormones*: Katherine E. Wynne-Edwards, "Why Do Some Men Experience Pregnancy Symptoms Such as Vomiting and Nausea When Their Wives Are Pregnant?" *Scientific American*, June 28, 2004, www.scientificamerican.com/article.cfm?id=why-do-some-men-experienc.

74 *They recruited thirty-four couples*: Anne E. Storey et al., "Hormonal Correlates of Paternal Responsiveness in New and Expectant Fathers," *Evolution and Human Behavior* 21, no. 2 (2000): 79–95.

75 *testosterone was highest in fathers who*: Jennifer S. Mascaro, Patrick D. Hacketta, and James K. Rilling, "Testicular Volume Is Inversely Correlated with Nurturing-Related Brain Activity in Human Fathers," *Proceedings of the National Academy of Sciences*, early online edition, Sept. 4, 2013, www.pnas.org/content/early/2013/09/04/1305579110.

75 *This relationship is seen in animals*: Sarah Zhang, "Better Fathers Have Smaller Testicles," *Nature News*, Sept. 9, 2013, www.nature.com/news/better-fathers-have-smaller-testicles-1.13701.

76 *More than hormones are at work*: Prakesh S. Shah and Knowledge Synthesis Group, "Paternal Factors and Low Birthweight, Preterm, and Small for Gestational Age Births: A Systematic Review," *American Journal of Obstetrics and Gynecology* 202, no. 2 (2010): 103–23.

78 *fathers who were involved with their partners*: "Father Involvement in Pregnancy Could Reduce Infant Mortality," EurekAlert, June 17, 2010, www.eurekalert.org/pub_releases/2010-06/uosf-fii061710.php.

78 *affect the birth weight of their children*: Lesley M. E. McCowan et al., "Paternal Contribution to Small for Gestational Age Babies: A Multicenter Prospective Study," *Obesity* 19, no. 5 (2011): 1035–39.

79 *Bowlby began his work*: Sarah Blaffer Hrdy, *Mothers and Others: The Evolutionary Origins of Mutual Understanding* (Cambridge, MA: Harvard University Press, 2009), 82.

80 *Freud was not a scientist*: Anthony Storr, *Freud: A Very Short Introduction* (Oxford: Oxford University Press, 1989), 146. J. Allan Hobson and Jonathan A. Leonard, *Out of Its Mind: Psychiatry in Crisis: A Call for Reform* (New York: Basic Books, 2001).

83 *evidence for the adverse consequences of depression*: Anne Lise Kvalevaag et al., "Paternal Mental Health and Socioemotional and Behavioral Development in their Children," *Pediatrics* 131, no. 2 (2013): e463–69, http://pediatrics.aappublications.org/content/131/2/e463.full.pdf.

84 *paternal depression was indeed a risk factor*: Laurie Barclay, "Paternal Depressive Symptoms During Pregnancy May Predict Excessive Infant Crying," Medscape, July 10, 2009, www.medscape.org/viewarticle/705633; Mijke P. van den Berg et al., "Paternal Depressive Symptoms During Pregnancy Are Related to Excessive Infant Crying," *Pediatrics* 124, no. 1 (2009), www.pediatricsdigest.mobi/content/124/1/e96.full; R. Neal Davis et al., "Fathers' Depression Related to Positive and Negative Parenting Behaviors with 1-Year-Old Children," *Pediatrics* 127, no. 4 (2011): 612–18, http://pediatrics.aappublications.org/content/127/4/612.full.

85 *Families Through Time*: James P. McHale, *Charting the Bumpy Road of Coparenthood: Understanding the Challenges of Family Life* (Washington, DC: Zero to Three, 2007), 2, 30, 56–57, 61.

87 *Fathers who are involved during pregnancy*: Natasha J. Cabrera et al., "Explaining the Long Reach of Fathers' Prenatal Involvement on Later Paternal Engagement," *Journal of Marriage and Family* 70, no. 5 (2008): 1094, www.ncbi.nlm.nih.gov/pmc/articles/PMC2822357.

88 *When expectant fathers are asked*: Cowan and Cowan, *When Partners Become Parents*, 97.

89 *The researchers tried offering their program*: Philip A. Cowan et al., "Promoting Fathers' Engagement with Children: Preventive Interventions for Low-Income Families," *Journal of Marriage and Family* 71, no. 3 (2009): 663–79.

4. FATHERS IN THE LAB: OF MICE AND MEN

94 *tested rats' ability to discriminate*: Allison L. Foote and Jonathon D. Crystal, "Metacognition in the Rat," *Current Biology* 17, no. 6 (2007): 551–55, www.tinyurl.com/k7tupky.

95 *developed enhanced spatial learning and memory*: Craig Howard Kinsley and Kelly G. Lambert, "The Maternal Brain," *Scientific American*,

January 2006, www.scientificamerican.com/article.cfm?id=the-maternal
-brain.

96 *paternal grooming is essential*: James P. Curley, "Parent-of-Origin Effects on Parental Behavior," in Robert S. Bridges, ed., *Neurobiology of the Parental Brain* (Amsterdam: Elsevier, 2008), 326.

106 *"The male allows the egg to fall gently to the ice"*: Jeffrey Moussaieff Masson, *The Emperor's Embrace* (New York: Washington Square Press, 1999), 26–28.

107 *The seahorse takes a far more bizarre route*: Ibid., 68–69.

107 *nasty example of parental favoritism*: Natalie Angier, "Paternal Bonds, Special and Strange," *New York Times*, June 14, 2010, www.nytimes.com /2010/06/15/science/15fath.html?pagewanted=all.

108 *In some species of poison frogs*. Hanna Kokko and Michael Jennions, "Behavioural Ecology: Ways to Raise Tadpoles," *Nature* 464 (2010): 990.

108 *The male midwife toad carries strings*: Masson, *Emperor's Embrace*, 74–75.

108 *a nod to marmosets and tamarins*: David P. Barash and Judith Eve Lipton, *Strange Bedfellows: The Surprising Connection Between Sex, Evolution and Monogamy* (New York: Bellevue Literary Press, 2009), 73–76.

108 *cotton-top tamarin fathers start carrying*: Sofia Refetoff Zahed et al., "Social Dynamics and Individual Plasticity of Infant Care Behavior in Cooperatively Breeding Cotton-Top Tamarins," *American Journal of Primatology* 72, no. 4 (2009): 296.

109 *showed that in a frightening situation*: Karen M. Kostan and Charles T. Snowdon, "Attachment and Social Preferences in Cooperatively-Reared Cotton-Top Tamarins," *American Journal of Primatology* 57, no. 3 (2002): 131–39, www.ncbi.nlm.nih.gov/pmc/articles/PMC1482833.

109 *exiled when childbirth moved out of the home*: Judith Walzer Leavitt, *Make Room for Daddy: The Journey from Waiting Room to Birthing Room* (Chapel Hill: University of North Carolina Press, 2009), 1–7, 8, 161–63, 231–33, 236, 242–43, 245, 259, 260, 261, 266.

113 *Humans are predominantly monogamous*: Masson, *Emperor's Embrace*, 53.

113 *"combines short-term and long-term mating bonds"*: Bernard Chapais, "Monogamy, Strongly Bonded Groups, and the Evolution of Human Social Structure," *Evolutionary Anthropology* 22, no. 2 (2013): 52–65.

114 *graceful example of harmony and monogamy*: Barash and Lipton, *Strange Bedfellows*, 28–29.

114 *likely dates back to the dinosaurs*: David J. Varricchio et al., "Avian Paternal Care Had Dinosaur Origin," *Science* 322 (2008): 1826–28, www .esf.edu/EFB/faculty/documents/varricchio2008paternalcaredinosours .pdf.

115 *are increasingly seeking paternity tests*: Ruth Padawer, "Who Knew I Was Not the Father?" *New York Times*, Nov. 17, 2009, www.nytimes .com/2009/11/22/magazine/22Paternity-t.html?pagewanted=all.

115 *a wandering male cannot justify his infidelity*: Barash and Lipton, *Strange Bedfellows*, 53.

116 *males can be coaxed to rise*: Stephen J. Suomi, interview with the author, March 11, 2011.

117 *"One of the most striking aspects"*: William K. Redican and G. Mitchell, "Play Between Adult Male and Infant Rhesus Monkeys," *American Zoologist* 14, no. 1 (1974): 295–302.

118 *one in ten new fathers suffers*: Charlene Laino, "Men Also Get Postpartum Depression," WebMD, May 6, 2008, www.webmd.com/depression /postpartum-depression/news/20080506/men-also-get-postpartum -depression.

118 *linked to conduct problems or hyperactivity*: Michael E. Lamb, ed., *The Role of the Father in Child Development*, 5th ed. (Hoboken, NJ: Wiley, 2010), 107–108.

5. INFANTS: SCULPTING FATHERS' BRAINS

122 *Salvador Minuchin, whose book*: James P. McHale, *Charting the Bumpy Road of Coparenthood: Understanding the Challenges of Family Life* (Washington, DC: Zero to Three, 2007), 5.

123 *think about various roles in their lives*: Carolyn Pape Cowan and Philip A. Cowan, *When Partners Become Parents: The Big Life Change for Couples* (New York: Basic Books, 1992), 80–82.

125 *Kotelchuck did four studies*: Michael E. Lamb, ed., *The Role of the Father in Child Development*, 5th ed. (Hoboken, NJ: Wiley, 2010), 96.

127 *fathers often show the same elation*: Ibid., 97.

127 *Fathers also pick up on cues*: Sarah Blaffer Hrdy, *Mothers and Others: The Evolutionary Origins of Mutual Understanding* (Cambridge, MA: Harvard University Press, 2009), 42.

127 *a unique response to their babies' cries*: James E. Swain and Jeffrey P. Lorberbaum, "Imaging the Human Parental Brain," in *Neurobiology of the Parental Brain* (Amsterdam: Elsevier, 2008), 84.

131 *only in the past few centuries that health care*: Marian F. MacDorman, Donna L. Hoyert, and T. J. Mathew, "Recent Declines in Infant Mortality in the United States, 2005–2011," National Center for Health Statistics data brief no. 120 (April 2013), www.cdc.gov/nchs/data/databriefs /db120.htm.

131 *Anxiety in new parents and obsessive-compulsive*: James F. Leckman, "Early Parental Preoccupations and Behaviors and Their Possible Relationship to the Symptoms of Obsessive-Compulsive Disorder," *Acta Psychiatrica Scandinavica* 100, Supplement S396 (1999): 1–26.

132 *breast-feeding mothers showed greater brain response*: Pilyoung Kim et al., "Breastfeeding, Brain Activation to Own Infant Cry, and Maternal Sensitivity," *Journal of Child Psychology and Psychiatry* 52, no. 8 (2011): 907–15.

132 *increased activity in the prefrontal cortex*: James F. Swain, "Parenting and Neural Plasticity in Fathers' Brains" (unpublished study), personal communication, March 26, 2013.

134 *She enlisted one hundred Israeli couples*: Ruth Feldman, "Infant-Mother and Infant-Father Synchrony: The Coregulation of Positive Arousal," *Infant Mental Health Journal* 24, no. 1 (2003): 1–23, www.tinyurl.com/nyfeypl.

135 *men who take time off from work*: Lamb, *Role of the Father*, 5th ed., 97–98.

135 *referred to as fragile families*: Natasha J. Cabrera et al., "Explaining the Long Reach of Fathers' Prenatal Involvement on Later Paternal Engagement," *Journal of Marriage and Family* 70, no. 5 (2008): 1094, www.ncbi .nlm.nih.gov/pmc/articles/PMC2822357.

136 *the researchers recruited fifty six couples*: Liat Tikotzky et al., "Infant Sleep and Paternal Involvement in Infant Caregiving During the First 6 Months of Life," *Journal of Pediatric Psychology* 36, no. 1 (2010): 36–46.

137 *can include tantrums, biting, and kicking*: Paul G. Ramchandani et al., "Do Early Father-Infant Interactions Predict the Onset of Externalizing Behaviours in Young Children?" *Journal of Child Psychology and Psychiatry* 54, no. 1 (2013): 56–64, www.ncbi.nlm.nih.gov/pmc/articles /PMC3562489.

138 *looked at 624 men in Cebu*: Lee T. Gettler et al., "Longitudinal Evidence That Fatherhood Decreases Testosterone in Human Males," *PNAS* 108, no. 39 (2011): 16194–99, www.ncbi.nlm.nih.gov/pmc/articles/PMC 3182719.

139 *topical testosterone can be dangerous*: "Safety Concerns About Testosterone Gel," WebMD, www.webmd.com/fda/safety-concerns-about-testosterone-gel.

139 *biology behind father-infant attachments*: Patty X. Kuo et al., "Neural Responses to Infants Linked with Behavioral Interactions and Testosterone in Fathers," *Biological Psychology* 91, no. 2 (2012): 302–306.

6. CHILDREN: LANGUAGE, LEARNING, AND *BATMAN*

143 *From World War II through the 1960s*: Michael E. Lamb, ed., *The Role of the Father in Child Development*, 5th ed. (Hoboken, NJ: Wiley, 2010), 4–5.

143 *toughness, power, status, sturdiness*: Michael Kimmel, *Guyland: The Perilous World Where Boys Become Men* (New York: Harper, 2008), 45–46.

144 *looking at children's language development*: Nadya Pancsofar and Lynne Vernon-Feagans, "Fathers' Early Contributions to Children's Language Development in Families from Low-Income Rural Communities," *Early Childhood Research Quarterly* 25, no. 4 (2010): 450–63.

147 *a boost in children's intellectual development*: Catherine S. Tamis-LeMonda et al., "Fathers and Mothers at Play With Their 2- and 3-Year-Olds: Contributions to Language and Cognitive Development," *Child Development* 75, no. 6 (2004): 1806–20, www.popcenter.umd.edu /filab/publications/images-firg/tamis%20lemonda%20shannon%20cabrera %20lamb%202004.pdf.

147 *wealthier fathers produced a greater rise*: Daniel Nettle, "Why Do Some Dads Get More Involved Than Others? Evidence from a Large British Cohort," *Evolution and Human Behavior* 29 (2008): 416–23, www.staff .ncl.ac.uk/daniel.nettle/ehb%20paternal%20investment.pdf.

148 *fathers' influence over children's intellectual development*: Erin Pougnet et al., "Fathers' Influence on Children's Cognitive and Behavioural Functioning: A Longitudinal Study of Canadian Families," *Canadian Journal of Behavioural Science* 43, no. 3 (2011): 173–82.

148 *think of their fathers as playmates*: Michael E. Lamb, ed., *The Role of the Father in Child Development*, 4th ed. (Hoboken, NJ: Wiley, 2004), 254.

148 *"Fathers often use objects in an incongruous way"*: Daniel Paquette, "Theorizing the Father-Child Relationship: Mechanisms and Developmental Outcomes," *Human Development* 47, no. 4 (2004): 205.

150 *related to children's transition to school*: National Institute of Child Health and Human Development Early Child Care Research Network,

"Fathers' and Mothers' Parenting Behavior and Beliefs as Predictors of Children's Social Adjustment in the Transition to School," *Journal of Family Psychology* 18, no. 4 (2004): 628–38.

150 *more parental leave for fathers*: Anna Sarkadi et al., "Fathers' Involvement and Children's Developmental Outcomes: A Systematic Review of Longitudinal Studies," *Acta Paediatrica* 97 (2008): 153–58, www.rikshand boken-bhv.se/Dokument/Sarkadi_fathersinvolvement.pdf.

151 *new relationships and friendships*: University of California, Riverside, Department of Psychology, Ross D. Parke biography, http://psych.ucr .edu/faculty/parke/index.html.

151 *children whose fathers were away at war*: Ross D. Parke, "Fathering and Children's Peer Relationships," in Lamb, *Role of the Father*, 4th ed., 309.

152 *watched fathers in their homes playing*: Ibid., 312.

153 *sensitive to the needs and feelings*: Ibid.

153 *Fathers' work schedules were*: S. L. Champion et al., "Parental Work Schedules and Child Overweight and Obesity," *International Journal of Obesity* 36, no. 4 (2012): 573–80.

154 *Fathers' smoking has been associated*: Man Ki Kwok et al., "Paternal Smoking and Childhood Overweight: Evidence from the Hong Kong 'Children of 1997,'" *Pediatrics* 126, no. 1 (2009): e46–e56, www.pediatrics digest.mobi/content/126/1/e46.full.

155 *"Who Keeps Children Alive?"*: Rebecca Sear and Ruth Mace, "Who Keeps Children Alive?: A Review of the Effects of Kin on Child Survival," *Evolution and Human Behavior* 29, no. 1 (2008): 1–18, http://evo lution.binghamton.edu/evos/wp-content/uploads/2010/09/who keeps .pdf.

7. TEENAGERS: ABSENCE, PUBERTY, AND FAITHFUL VOLES

159 *departed from the usual formality*: Danielle J. DelPriore and Sarah E. Hill, "The Effects of Paternal Disengagement on Women's Sexual Decision Making: An Experimental Approach," *Journal of Personality and Social Psychology* 105, no. 2 (2013): 234–46.

159 *the disturbing rate of teen pregnancy*: James Eng, "90 Pregnancies at One High School," NBC News, Jan. 14, 2011, http://usnews.nbcnews .com/_news/2011/01/14/5841767-90-pregnancies-at-one-high-school ?lite.

162 *His work on fathers began in the late 1990s*: Bruce J. Ellis, telephone interview with the author, Aug. 7, 2013.

162 *"set" the reproductive strategy*: Jay Belsky, "Childhood Experience and the Development of Reproductive Strategies," *Psicothema* 22, no. 1 (1991): 28–34, www.tinyurl.com/luo3o2s.

163 *a "quasi-experiment"*: Jacqueline M. Tither and Bruce J. Ellis, "Impact of Fathers on Daughters' Age at Menarche: A Genetically and Environmentally Controlled Sibling Study," *Developmental Psychology* 44, no. 5 (2008): 1409–20, http://cals.arizona.edu/fcs/sites/cals.arizona.edu.fcs /files/DP%20Tither_Ellis%202008.pdf.

167 *One of the best animals for exploring*: Kate Egan, "Love and Sex: The Vole Story," *Emory Medicine*, Summer 1998, http://whsc.emory.edu/_pubs /em/1998summer/vole.html.

168 *one of the key factors underlying vole behavior*: Larry J. Young, TEDx-Emory talk, April 20, 2013, www.youtube.com/watch?v=EoweLVvR7-8 #at=401.

168 *brains of prairie and montane voles*: Thomas R. Insel and Lawrence E. Shapiro, "Oxytocin Receptor Distribution Reflects Social Organization in Monogamous and Polygamous Voles," *PNAS* 89 (1992): 5981–85, www .ncbi.nlm.nih.gov/pmc/articles/PMC402122/pdf/pnas01087-0291.pdf.

169 *describes as "mind-blowing"*: Young, TEDxEmory talk.

169 *whether the boost in vasopressin receptors*: Miranda M. Lim et al., "Enhanced Partner Preference in a Promiscuous Species by Manipulating the Expression of a Single Gene," *Nature* 429 (2004): 754–57.

171 *looked at hormonal changes in voles*: William M. Kenkel et al., "Neuroendocrine and Behavioural Responses to Exposure to an Infant in Male Prairie Voles," *Journal of Neuroendocrinology* 24, no. 6 (2012): 874–86.

171 *The pups raised without a father displayed*: Rui Jia et al., "Effects of Neonatal Paternal Deprivation or Early Deprivation on Anxiety and Social Behaviors of the Adults in Mandarin Voles," *Behavioural Processes* 82, no. 3 (2009): 271–78.

172 *a particular vasopressin receptor gene*: Hasse Walum et al., "Genetic Variation in the Vasopressin Receptor 1a Gene (AVPR1A) Associates with Pair-Bonding Behavior in Humans," *PNAS* 105, no. 37 (2008): 14153–56.

172 *variations in an oxytocin receptor gene*: Hasse Walum et al., "Variation in the Oxytocin Receptor Gene (OXTR) Is Associated with Pair-Bonding and Social Behavior," *Biological Psychiatry* 71, no. 5 (2012): 419–26.

173 *it can reduce stress, encourage trust*: Peter A. Bos et al., "Acute Effects of Steroid Hormones and Neuropeptides on Human Social-Emotional Behavior: A Review of Single Administration Studies," *Frontiers in Neuroendocrinology* 33, no. 1 (2012): 17–35, doi:10.1016/j.yfrne.2011.01.002.

173 *each father was given a whiff of oxytocin*: Fabienne Naber et al., "Intranasal Oxytocin Increases Fathers' Observed Responsiveness During Play with Their Children: A Double-Blind Within-Subject Experiment," *Psychoneuroendocrinology* 35, no. 10 (2010), 1583–86, www.marinusvan ijzendoorn.nl/wp-content/uploads/2012/07/NaberVanIJzendoornDes champsetal2010PNECoxytocinincreasesfathersobservedresponsiveness .pdf.

174 *provided high levels of affectionate contact*": Ruth Feldman et al., "Natural Variations in Maternal and Paternal Care Are Associated with Systematic Changes in Oxytocin Following Parent-Infant Contact," *Psychoneuroendocrinology* 35, no. 8 (2010), www.utm.utoronto.ca/~crpl /downloads/Feldman/Oxytocin%20PNEC%202010%20final.pdf.

175 *their ability to interact socially with others*: Omri Weisman et al., "Oxytocin Administration to Parent Enhances Infant Physiological and Behavioral Readiness for Social Engagement," *Biological Psychiatry* 72, no. 12 (2012): 982–89, http://dx.doi.org/10.1016/j.biopsych.2012.06.011.

175 *prolactin has an important role to play*: Ilanit Gordon et al., "Prolactin, Oxytocin, and the Development of Paternal Behavior Across the First Six Months of Fatherhood," *Hormones and Behavior* 58, no. 3 (2010): 513–18, www.ncbi.nlm.nih.gov/pmc/articles/PMC3247300.

176 *the work on oxytocin and relationships*: Ruth Feldman, "Oxytocin and Social Affiliation in Humans," *Hormones and Behavior* 61 (2012): 380–91, www.tinyurl.com/kv7jd64.

176 *how parenting influences risky sexual behavior*: Rebekah Levine Coley et al., "Fathers' and Mothers' Parenting Predicting and Responding to Adolescent Sexual Risk Behaviors," *Child Development* 80, no. 3 (2009): 808–27, doi:10.1111/j.1467-8624.2009.01299.x.

177 *sons of teenage fathers were 1.8 times more likely*: Heather Sipsma et al., "Like Father, Like Son: The Intergenerational Cycle of Adolescent Fatherhood," *American Journal of Public Health* 100, no. 3 (2010): 517–24.

178 *consequences for children who perceive themselves*: Abdul Khaleque and Ronald P. Rohner, "Transnational Relations Between Perceived Parental Acceptance and Personality Dispositions of Children and Adults: A Meta-Analytic Review," *Personality and Social Psychology Review* 16,

no. 2 (2012): 103–15, www.sakkyndig.com/psykologi/artvit/khaleque2012
.pdf.

179 *how much time their fathers spent with them*: Daniel Goleman, "Studies
on Development of Empathy Challenge Some Old Assumptions," *New
York Times*, July 12, 1990, www.nytimes.com/1990/07/12/us/health
-studies-on-development-of-empathy-challenge-some-old-assumptions
.html.

179 *handle the day-to-day stresses of adulthood*: American Psychological
Association, "Childhood Memories of Father Have Lasting Impact on
Men's Ability to Handle Stress," press release, Aug. 12, 2010, www.apa.org
/news/press/releases/2010/08/childhood-memories.aspx.

180 *activity in the caudate, a deep brain structure*: Marie Arsalidou et al.,
"Brain Responses Differ to Faces of Mothers and Fathers," *Brain and
Cognition* 74 (2010): 47–51, www.tinyurl.com/l4tnxsr.

8. OLDER FATHERS: THE REWARDS AND RISKS OF WAITING

181 *This confusion was wonderfully captured*: Nora Ephron and Delia
Ephron, *You've Got Mail*, Internet Movie Script Database, www.imsdb
.com/scripts/You%27ve-Got-Mail.html.

182 *the children of fathers forty and over*: Rebecca G. Smith et al., "Advancing Paternal Age Is Associated with Deficits in Social and Exploratory
Behaviors in the Offspring: A Mouse Model," *PLoS One* 4, no. 12 (2009),
www.plosone.org/article/info%3Adoi%2F10.1371%2Fjournal.pone
.0008456.

183 *associated with an increased risk of schizophrenia*: Abraham Reichenberg et al., "Advancing Paternal Age and Autism," *Archives of General
Psychiatry* 63, no. 9 (2006): 1026–32, http://archpsyc.jamanetwork.com
/article.aspx?articleid=668208.

183 *I called the U.S. Census Bureau*: U.S. Census Bureau, "Father's Day:
June 16, 2013," www.prnewswire.com/news-releases/census-bureau-pro
file-america-facts-for-features-fathers-day-june-16-2013-203603321
.html.

184 *Information is available from birth certificates*: Stephanie Ventura, National Center for Health Statistics, personal communication, Jan. 15,
2007.

185 *fathers who are having their first child after age thirty-five*: Matthew
Weinshenker, personal communication, Sept. 15, 2006.

187 *the risk of dwarfism rose with the father's age*: James F. Crow, "Hardy, Weinberg and Language Impediments," in "Perspectives: Anecdotal, Historical and Critical Commentaries on Genetics," edited by J. F. Crow and William F. Dove, *Genetics* 152 (1999): 821–25, www.genetics.org /content/152/3/821.full.pdf.

187 *women whose partners are thirty-five or older*: Mailman School of Public Health, Columbia University, "Higher Paternal Age Associated with Increased Rates of Miscarriage," *At the Frontline* 1, no. 5 (Nov. 2006), www.mailmanschool.org/e-newsletter/AtTheFrontline-vol1no5/r-Paternal AgeMiscarriage.html.

192 *Autism spectrum disorders occurred at a rate*: Reichenberg et al., "Advancing Paternal Age and Autism."

193 *looked at the genetics of older fathers*: Sukanta Saha et al., "Advanced Paternal Age Is Associated with Impaired Neurocognitive Outcomes During Infancy and Childhood," *PLoS Medicine* 6, no. 3 (2009): e1000040, www.plosmedicine.org/article/info:doi/10.1371/journal.pmed .1000040.

194 *3,443 patients with intellectual disabilities*: Jayne Y. Hehir-Kwa et al., "De Novo Copy Number Variants Associated with Intellectual Disability Have a Paternal Origin and Age Bias," *Journal of Medical Genetics* 48, no. 11 (2011): 776–78, http://autismdialogues.blogspot.com/2011/10/de -novo-copy-number-variants-associated.html.

194 *bred female mice with older males*: Reichenberg et al., "Advancing Paternal Age and Autism."

196 *rise in autism is due to the growing number of older fathers*: deCODE Genetics, "Science," www.dcode.com/research.

196 *how many new cases of autism could arise as the consequence*: Augustine Kong et al., "Rate of De Novo Mutations, Father's Age, and Disease Risk," *Nature* 488 (2012): 471–75, www.ncbi.nlm.nih.gov/pmc/articles/PMC 3548427.

197 *the cause of 20 to 30 percent of all cases of autism*: Benedict Carey, "Father's Age Is Linked to Risk of Autism and Schizophrenia," *New York Times*, Aug. 22, 2012, www.nytimes.com/2012/08/23/health/fathers-age -is-linked-to-risk-of-autism-and-schizophrenia.html?_r=0.

199 *The American College of Medical Genetics notes the risks*: Helga V. Toriello and Jeanne M. Meck, "Statement on Guidance for Genetic Counseling in Advanced Paternal Age," *Genetics in Medicine*, 10, no. 6 (2008): 457–60.

199 *two past presidents of the American College of Medical Genetics*: Charles J. Epstein and Marilyn C. Jones, telephone interviews with the author, Jan. 30, 2007 (Epstein) and Jan. 28, 2007 (Jones).

200 *"They should be revealing information"*: Arthur L. Caplan, telephone interview with the author, Jan. 31, 2007.

201 *"It's going to be more and more of an issue"*: Herbert Y. Meltzer, telephone interview with the author, Jan. 30, 2007.

202 *telomeres shorten as we age*: Dan T. A. Eisenberg et al., "Delayed Paternal Age of Reproduction in Humans Is Associated with Longer Telomeres Across Two Generations of Descendants," *PNAS* 109, no. 26 (2012): 10251–56, www.pnas.org/content/109/26/10251.full.pdf.

203 *they can grow to be slightly taller and slimmer*: Kristina Fiore, "Dad's Age Tied to Kid's Weight, Height, LDL," MedPage Today, July 22, 2013, www.medpagetoday.com/Endocrinology/GeneralEndocrinology/40605.

9. WHAT FATHERS DO

207 *"is a human universal"*: Richard Wrangham, *Catching Fire: How Cooking Made Us Human* (New York: Basic Books, 2009), 130–35, 139, 146, 148–49, 150, 154, 177.

211 *Neanderthals developed cooking 200,000 years ago*: C. Loring Brace cited in Rachael Moeller Gorman, "Cooking Up Bigger Brains," *Scientific American*, Dec. 16, 2007, www.scientificamerican.com/article.cfm ?id=cooking-up-bigger-brains.

212 *In that long prehistoric era, fathers taught*: Barry S. Hewlett and Shane J. MacFarlan, "Fathers' Roles in Hunter-Gatherer and Other Small-Scale Cultures," in *The Role of the Father in Child Development*, 5th ed., edited by Michael E. Lamb (Hoboken, NJ: Wiley, 2010), 413–31.

212 *Changes in work and family life in the United States*: Kim Parker and Wendy Wang, "Modern Parenthood," PewResearch Social and Demographic Trends, Pew Research Center, March 14, 2013, www.pewsocial trends.org/2013/03/14/modern-parenthood-roles-of-moms-and-dads -converge-as-they-balance-work-and-family.

213 *men experience more conflict between work and family*: Ellen Galinsky et al., "Times Are Changing: Gender and Generation at Work and at Home," Families and Work Institute, 2008 (revised August 2011), www .familiesandwork.org/site/research/reports/Times_Are_Changing.pdf.

213 *Americans work longer hours*: Joan C. Williams and Heather Boushey, "The Three Faces of Work-Family Conflict: The Poor, the Professionals, and the Missing Middle," Center for American Progress, www.american progress.org/issues/labor/report/2010/01/25/7194/the-three-faces-of -work-family-conflict.

214 *they feel they're being pushed harder at work*: Kerstin Aumann et al., "The New Male Mystique," Families and Work Institute, www.families andwork.org/site/research/reports/newmalemystique.pdf.

214 *The difficulty that fathers face trying to fulfill*: Carolyn Pape Cowan and Philip A. Cowan, *When Partners Become Parents: The Big Life Change for Couples* (New York: Basic Books, 1992), 94, 104.

215 *some men are indeed strangely detached from their families.* Annette Lareau, "My Wife Can Tell Me Who I Know: Methodological and Conceptual Problems in Studying Fathers," *Qualitative Sociology* 23, no. 4 (2000): 407–33, www.jennyjvalentine.com/7900%20PDFS/My%20Wife%20Can %20Tell%20You%20Who%20I%20Know%20-%20Article.htm.pdf.

216 *Fathers also grapple with social attitudes*: Victoria L. Brescoll and Eric Luis Uhlmann, "Attitudes Toward Traditional and Nontraditional Parents," *Psychology of Women Quarterly* 29, no. 4 (2005): 436–45.

216 *many fathers take only some of their paternity leave*: Ibid., 440.

217 *what's often called maternal gatekeeping*: Sarah M. Allen and Alan J. Hawkins, "Maternal Gatekeeping: Mothers' Beliefs and Behaviors That Inhibit Greater Father Involvement in Family Work," *Journal of Marriage and Family* 61, no. 1 (1999): 199–212, www.jstor.org/stable/353894.

218 *"Some women both cherish and resent being"*: Sarah J. Schoppe Sullivan et al., "Maternal Gatekeeping, Coparenting Quality, and Fathering Behavior in Families with Infants," *Journal of Family Psychology* 22, no. 3 (2008): 389–98.

218 *They asked ninety-seven couples*: Ibid.

219 *downward spiral in marital satisfaction*: Cowan and Cowan, *When Partners Become Parents*, 16–22.

220 *question we should ask about father absence*: Paul R. Amato and Julie M. Sobolewski, "The Effects of Divorce on Fathers and Children," in *The Role of the Father in Child Development*, 4th ed., edited by Michael E. Lamb (Hoboken, NJ: Wiley, 2004), 348.

220 *children are born to parents who aren't married*: Mathematica Policy Research, "Building Strong Families," January 2005, www.mathematica -mpr.com/publications/PDFs/bsfisbr3.pdf.

220 *All the current figures are far higher*: Gretchen Livingston and Kim Parker, "A Tale of Two Fathers: More Are Active, but More Are Absent," PewResearch Social and Demographic Trends, Pew Research Center, June 15, 2011, www.pewsocialtrends.org/2011/06/15/a-tale-of-two-fathers.

220 *Fewer fathers are living with*: Amato and Sobolewski, "Effects of Divorce," in Lamb, *Role of the Father*, 4th ed., 353.

221 *fathers had little or no effect on mortality rates*: Peter B. Gray and Kermyt G. Anderson, *Fatherhood: Evolution and Human Paternal Behavior* (Cambridge, MA: Harvard University Press, 2010), 122.

221 *a major contributor to crime and juvenile delinquency*: Cynthia R. Daniels, ed., *Lost Fathers: The Politics of Fatherlessness in America* (New York: St. Martin's Press, 1998), 4.

222 *data linking fatherlessness to adverse consequences*: Ibid., 36.

222 *"on the whole, two parents—a father and a mother"*: David Popenoe, *Life Without Father: Compelling New Evidence That Fatherhood and Marriage Are Indispensable for the Good of Children and Society* (New York: Free Press, 1996), 147.

222 *The most important and immediate consequence*: Daniels, *Lost Fathers*, 36–39.

223 *Families with unmarried parents often defy*: Sara S. McLanahan and Marcia J. Carlson, "Welfare Reform, Fertility and Father Involvement," Center for Research on Child Wellbeing, working paper no. 01-13-FF, draft, Aug. 6, 2001, http://s3.amazonaws.com/zanran_storage/www.north western.edu/ContentPages/6513017.pdf.

225 *produce wiring changes in the brains of their pups*: Wladimir Ovtscharoff, Jr., et al., "Lack of Paternal Care Affects Synaptic Development in the Anterior Cingulate Cortex," *Brain Research* 1116, no. 1 (2006): 58–63, www.diyfather.com/files/paternal_care.pdf.

AFTERWORD: FATHERS MATTER

231 *"As a matter of fact, you do need"*: Alana S., "Taboos and the New Voiceless Americans," FamilyScholars.org, May 20, 2010, www.familyscholars .org/2010/05/20/taboos-and-the-new-voiceless-americans.

232 *"I don't buy it"*: Kyle D. Pruett, *Fatherneed: Why Father Care Is as Essential as Mother Care for Your Child* (New York: Free Press, 2000), 74.

232 *"The fathers' custody activists claim"*: National Organization for Women Foundation, Family Law Ad Hoc Advisory Committee, newsletter,

Fall 2012, www.nowfoundation.org/issues/family/FamilyLawNewsletter -Fall2012.pdf.

233 *"A father's involvement is crucial"*: "Fatherhood and Family Law: The Myths and the Facts," The Liz Library, www.thelizlibrary.org/site-index /site-index-frame.html#soulhttp://www.thelizlibrary.org/liz/017.htm.

233 *"If a person is not involved in the lives"*: Marcia A. Pappas, NOW–New York State, speaking on the Joint Custody Bill before the New York Senate, March 28, 2006, www.ancpr.com/2006/03/28/now-ny-speaks-on -joint-custody-bill.

234 *in which a worried father hands his car keys*: "Baby Driver," Subaru commercial, 2010, www.ispot.tv/ad/Y99V/subaru-baby-driver.

234 *a commercial that illustrates a father's role in play*: "Tide and Downy Presents: The Princess Dress," product commercial, 2013, www.youtube .com/watch?v=xCYwAOCLiTA.

Acknowledgments

While writing a book is often a solitary affair, I could not have written this one without the help of many scientists, friends, colleagues, and, of course, my family. My family and friends provided support and their own stories and experiences. And many of the researchers responsible for the important findings on fatherhood presented in this book took time from their own jobs to help me with mine. Without their guidance, I could never have put this story together.

I got the idea for *Do Fathers Matter?* in 2004, during a Journalism Fellowship in Child and Family Policy at the University of Maryland under the supervision of Carol Guensburg. I'd planned to write something about children, but the discussions with Carol and the other fellows led me to shift my focus to fathers—and I'm glad I did.

My agent, Beth Vesel, was a partner from the start. She helped shape the book when all I had was a long file of notes, clips, and scattered interviews. My editor at Scientific American/Farrar, Straus and Giroux, Amanda Moon, has been as excited about this book as I have, which made the process of editing and revising truly collaborative. She's smart, a sharp editor, scientifically literate—and nice. That's a rare combination. I could not have finished this book without Amanda's support and expertise.

Mariette DiChristina, the editor of *Scientific American*, enthusiastically supported the publication of *Do Fathers Matter?* under the Scientific American imprint of FSG. Kaja Perina, the editor of *Psychology Today*, gave me a comfortable home for *About Fathers*, my blog on the science of fatherhood. The wise counsel, connections, emotional support, and fellowship of the distinguished writers who make up the Invisible Institute in New York were invaluable.

Among the scientists who spent a lot of time with me explaining their work and saving me from potential errors were C. Sue Carter, Carolyn Pape Cowan, Philip A. Cowan, James P. Curley, Bruce J. Ellis, Catherine Franssen, David Gubernick, David Haig, Barry S. Hewlett, Sarah Hill, Michael E. Lamb, Kelly G. Lambert, Dolores Malaspina, James P. McHale, M. Azim Surani, James E. Swain, and Lynne Vernon-Feagans.

I also received help from Natasha J. Cabrera, Marcia Carlson, Catherine Dulac, Ruth Feldman, Ellen Galinsky, Jay Gingrich, Sara McLanahan, Herbert Y. Meltzer, Vicky Phares, Kyle D. Pruett, Abraham Reichenberg, Sarah J. Schoppe-Sullivan, Stephen J. Suomi, Myrna M. Weissman, and Richard Wrangham.

David Smith, a research librarian formerly at the New York Public Library, helped with my initial research. Tim Grahl of the Out:think Group helped me plan a social media strategy to reach the broadest possible audience with the book. Annie Gottlieb did a splendid job of not only copyediting the manuscript but also checking a lot of the scientific detail—and another set of eyes on that is always a good thing to have. Also helping with copyediting, proof-reading, and production at FSG were Mareike Grover, production editor, and Debra Helfand, managing editor.

My parents and my children provided an entirely different kind of help. My father and my mother showed me, by example, what it means to be a parent, and my children taught me everything else I needed to know. I'm afraid I am a slow learner, and I'm grateful to both my parents and my children for their patience.

I can't imagine how I could have written this book without the support, the editing and reediting, and the love of my wife, Elizabeth DeVita-Raeburn. Writing *is* a solitary affair—Elizabeth and I often communicate from room to room by e-mail—but she was with me all the way. That made the work much more satisfying, and truly enjoyable.

Index

A NOTE ABOUT THE AUTHOR

Paul Raeburn is the author of *Acquainted with the Night*, a memoir of raising children with depression and bipolar disorder, and the chief media critic for the Knight Science Journalism Tracker at MIT. He writes the *About Fathers* blog for *Psychology Today* and is a regular guest on NPR's *Science Friday*. Raeburn is a past president of the National Association of Science Writers and a former science editor at *BusinessWeek* and the Associated Press. He has written for *The New York Times*, *Discover*, *The Huffington Post*, and *Scientific American*, among many other publications. He lives in New York City with his wife and children. You can find him on Twitter at @dofathersmatter and @pracburn and on his website at www.paulraeburn.com.